WEALTHY HEALTHY MONEY

AND YOUR FINANCIAL LONG GAME

LILLIAN MEYERS

CFP®,CDFA®, EA

ISBN: 978-0-692-94399-1

Illustrations by James K. M. Watts

To Jerry, my husband of fifty-four years, without whom none of this would be possible.

-L. M.

Acknowledgements

I personally want to thank the many people who have touched my life and helped me toward my vision, my dreams, and my goals. I could never have done it alone. This book is the bringing together of many people who have helped me throughout my life: my God; my husband of 54 years, Jerry; Venita Van Castle CFP; Scott Keffer, coach mentor, Julia Leaven, a great wise woman; my parents, Milton and Andree; My Children Travis, Stacey and Elizabeth; and my sixth-grade teacher. (I wish I could remember her name. I do remember the color of her hair was dark brown, and it was curly and medium length; she was tall and very patient and loving, and she taught me how to read in English. If I had to do it over again, I would remember my teachers.)

Introduction

The dream of attaining wealth and freedom is global. Most everyone wants the freedom to do as we want and the wealth to have what we need for a happy life: a home, a quality education for children, a secure and flourishing retirement, a legacy and impact on our community and world.

You have the ability to accumulate wealth and achieve your dreams. All it takes is educating yourself on how to manage money and assets, a commitment to doing the work, and the mindset to see it through.

By creating a money strategy, you will be able to provide your family with security during your working years as well as create as a comfortable retirement. No one wants to live just a single pay check away from poverty. No one wants to live with nothing to fall back on. No one wants to be exposed to potential financial doom.

This book will help you make the right decisions that will take you to your vision and dreams. This will give you the power and confidence to create and maintain your plan. That said, there are no guarantees of success except what you personally achieve while using these tools and information as a guide.

This book is all about real world experiences and situations. I hope it will give you the information and guidance you need to build your future and the road map that will lead to your goals.

You do not need to read this cover to cover, page to page - all you need to do is ask, "What do I want to happen?" Then look it up. I recommend you start where you need the most help or have the most questions.

This book covers areas such as financial planning, insurance, education, taxes, retirement, legacy and estate, and much more to help you with decisions and to minimize financial mistakes.

Much of the technical information produced here can be

found on the web, and often, since there is no great way to improve upon technical language, particularly when it comes to insurance, investing and IRS rules. To keep information accurate, I quoted the web sites in question.

This book is a guide and a compilation to help put much of the information you need into one small document. From here, I encourage you to research on your own, check the primary sources for more information and further links (there is a resource list in the back of the book), make notes and seek a Certified Financial Planner for help. This is your start and a general overview. My goal is to help you navigate the sometimes contradictory information out there, and get a better idea of what you need to do to make sure you are as wealthy as you want, and as healthy as you can be.

1.

Where to Start

If you could paint your future, what would it look like?

Would it look like a Norman Rockwell picture of the perfect, ideal American life?

Or would it be like a Jackson Pollock painting, full of colors and exciting lines, and maybe a little out of control?

If you could have anything you wanted right now and

you could put together everything that you've worked for to ensure that lifestyle in the future, what would that look like? What are your vision and dreams?

Edward Hopper said, "Great art is the outward expression of an inner life of the artist, and this inner life will result in his personal vision of the world." You are the artist of your life. So, what is the outward expression of your inner life? What is the vision of the world you want to be a part of?

Close your eyes and dream big. As Yogi Berra said, "If you don't know where you're going, you probably won't get there." The vision needs to be clear and long term and with the end in mind. Mapping out your life plan is like planning a trip. We know where we want to go; now we need to pick the best route. The first thing Google Maps requires is the address of the final destination. From there, you can choose the route. Are you taking the shortest route, or are you taking the longest? Do you need rest stops along the way? Does this route lead directly to the destination?

Where exactly is that destination? Are you heading to the tropics? The Riviera? Do you own your own business? Do you have multiple advanced degrees? Do you live in a big house with an expansive view or a small apartment close to the action in New York? Really, where do you want to be? Or are you already here?

In 1967, my husband and I were at a crossroad. We were considering many options, even a move from the US to Australia. Jerry brought home pamphlets all about the country and what they were offering. Australia is not only beautiful, but we would get land for free if we were willing to relocate. The country needed skilled workers. Jerry was a journeyman and skilled worker, so it looked like Australia was a great opportunity. We considered it, prayed about it, and read everything we could about the offer. The one reason we did not go was we would have had to give up our American citizenship, and we were not prepared to do that. This was not part of our vision. Jerry and I grew up in foreign countries and giving up our citizenship was not a risk we were willing to take.

We all need to weigh the risks and rewards when we make decisions about our lives. Risk can be scary. But without risk, there is no possible way to earn the reward.

We also considered moving to Wyoming. We drove through the state. What a beautiful place! Half way through the drive, we had to stop to rest. We slept in the car. The next morning, we woke up at 7:00 AM to find the car doors had frozen closed. In the middle of June. Well, that killed that. It was much too cold for me and my family. Besides the cold, wages in the utility business (an industry in which Jerry had worked for six years) were too low. We discovered that in winter, workers could be released with no pay as early as 11:00 AM or when the temperature plummeted to 11 degrees. This was not part of our dream either, and so we moved on.

We checked out St. Louis and Pennsylvania where we had family. Both places featured extreme weather shifts and low-paying work. Obviously, not the best combination.

Finally, we drove into Northern California and felt we had landed in paradise. And here is where we made our home.

Dreams are important, but do your research.

You can even think small. Consider your car. Are you driving your dream car? If not, what is your dream car? What does it smell like? Does it have leather seats, special communication system, audio and video systems, special wheels. Do you look fantastic driving this beautiful car? Go to the dealership, take a look at your dream car. Sit in it. Where will this car take you? All over the country or just down the street?

What impact do you want to make? What is your passion? Do you want to save children? Save whales? Save trees? Do you want to cure cancer, feed the world, save the planet, stop human trafficking? Are your passion animals, large like elephants or small like cats and birds?

In 1999 my daughter Stacey and I traveled to Paris, Florence, Venice and Rome. We traveled by air; what excitement! Such a dream and accomplishment! Except the flight was not a dream come true. We sat in the very middle of a Boeing 777 - worst seats ever. We had to climb over someone every time we needed to use the toilet. It was a red-eye, and we were watching a movie while the flight attendants were taking turns napping in the back. The film was a comedy so, of course, the passengers were all laughing out loud, but the flight attendants kept shushing us. To this day, I wonder why they showed this funny movie if they needed to sleep.

On our way home, it was just as bad. Remembering all the pain and discomfort, I promised myself never to fly coach again. So, for me, success and wealth looked like flying first class. What is your story? What pain did you endure that inspired change? What will you never do again, and what will you always do from now on?

Even though we learned that "Money is the root of all evil" (1 Timothy 6:10), the Bible really refers to how the love of money, temptation, and greed can take over your life. Money has a lot of power. It can influence people, movies, businesses, and politics with both good and bad outcomes. Money is king; it opens doors for education, provides freedom of choice, empowers you, and moves you towards a better life. Money gives you the ability to have options in life, to fulfill your dreams, and to impact your world for the good of humanity.

In the song “Buy Me a Boat,” Chris Janson sings “I ain’t rich, but I damn sure want to be… money can’t buy everything… but it could buy me a boat.” Money can get you what you want.

So, money is tied to your dreams and goals.

But how to make it all work out in the end? Well, once you have your goals, you make a plan. The plan is all about small steps and incremental, achievable goals. Your dream, for example, could be to have $1,000,000 in the bank by age 40.

Let’s break that down:

First of all, what is a million? What does a million even look like? A million dollars is $1,000 times 1,000 - not difficult to do in your lifetime.

So how do you reach your first $1,000,000? Again, start small and start early. You can go to http://www.bankrate.com/calculators/savings/save-million-calculator.aspx, and calculate how to reach your saving goals. There are many more online calculators to help you with this goal.

If you have not saved anything at the age of 40, you will need $1,270 monthly at 7% yield (calculating inflation at 3%) to reach your goal at age 65 of $1,000,000. However, if you had started at age 25, you would only need $403 a month to reach the same goal.

Time is the difference. You could always try for 8% but remember, the higher the yield, the higher the risk. Risk and returns must work together so you don't want to take on risk that is out of proportion to the reward.

A Certified Financial Planner ™ (CFP®) that has a holistic approach. As a CFP®, I have found this is the best approach to work with people since it looks at the person's entire life and lifestyle. Holistic does not just look at individual parts of Financial Planning it uses the whole economic, social, environment, values, family and life of the person.

"There's no time like the present, no present like time," said Georgie Bying.

2.

Life Styles - Life Cycles

Your lifestyle today will determine your retirement style tomorrow.

Your current spending habits are crucial to your long-term success and to whether or not you reach your goals.

Is the life (style) you are living right now aligned with what you envision for your future? Are you on track to reach your dreams? Any dreams? You may be spending more than you have, and as a result, instead of saving for your dreams, you are inadvertently ransoming your future.

One of the first thing to examine is your career. Aside from the very large issue of whether or not you love your work, and aside from the very large issue of following your dreams, there are practical considerations when evaluating a job.

Working conditions

An indifferent job can be made more interesting by the benefits your company provides. Are you happy with your co-workers? When you take a look at your job, consider the teams you work with and your daily interactions - it's not trivial. They can provide a sense of belonging, create a feeling of home, and encourage self-esteem.

Compensation

Are you paid what you're worth? Have you checked online to make sure your compensation is compatible with the skills you have? Make sure your pay is in line with your work. This is true for both independent contractors as well as employees. Do not under value yourself and your skills. Make sure your salary is what it should be by visiting the U.S. Labor Statistic at www.bls.gov If you have decided to start your own business, check local prices and what can the economy handle.

Taxes

Are you a W-2 employee so your taxes are set aside by your employer, or are you a 1099 Miscellaneous non-employee with no taxes pulled from your checks? Be careful of the 1099 status. You may have to pay taxes come April because nothing has been set aside during the year. It is worth contacting an Enrolled Agent (EA) or a Certified Public Accountant (CPA) to find out and have it checked before you start the job; this will give you an idea where you will stand at the end of the year. One of the biggest advantages of working is, of course, the ability to save now for later, not to spend more later on taxes.

Save for Rain

Saving for a rainy day means you can cover no less than three months of expenses in case of an emergency. Preferably you can cover six months to ensure enough time to search for a new and better opportunity. Benjamin Franklin said it's not how much money you make, it's how much you keep.

When to begin to save? Now! It does not matter what age you start, just start now. If you are in your 20s and just starting to work, saving for retirement may seem insane in the face of needing a better car or a home. Are you still paying student debt? Even with that burden of student debt, if you are a full-time employee, there are easy ways to start saving. Acting during these years will be crucial for your later success.

The biggest advantage a 20-year-old saver has over anyone else is your age. You have time on your side, and time means compound interest. You can start very small and in the end, realize very big returns.

Start saving small amounts from each pay check, 3-4% at first. If your company offers a 401(k), Simple IRA, or SEP IRA make sure you know what your opportunities are for you and your family. Always use a percentage not dollars. A percentage will allow for the number of dollars you invest to grow as your salary or your income increases. So, plan to make more money in the future and get in the habit of saving a percentage of that amount, not a fixed amount. You want everything, including your savings and investments, to grow.

Strive to reach the maximum contribution levels of your employer's offered retirement plan. Generally, by ERISA and tax law, it will be 18% or higher of gross pay depending how your employer set up your plan. Check with your HR (Human Resources) department and get the package that explains your benefits.

Aim for $300,000 in retirement. $300,000 is manageable and attainable as well as believable. Then go for your next $300,000 and next $300,000. It is never too late to start; you will be ahead no matter when.

Why does saving now, in your twenties, make so much sense? “Compound interest is the eighth wonder of the world.” - Albert Einstein. If you start now, your savings will increase at a greater rate than if you wait until your thirties or forties to start to save. When you invest the money in the stock market, you should consider risk and returns. The stock market is a long-term activity. Work with the time you have, and when you are 22, you have a lot of time.

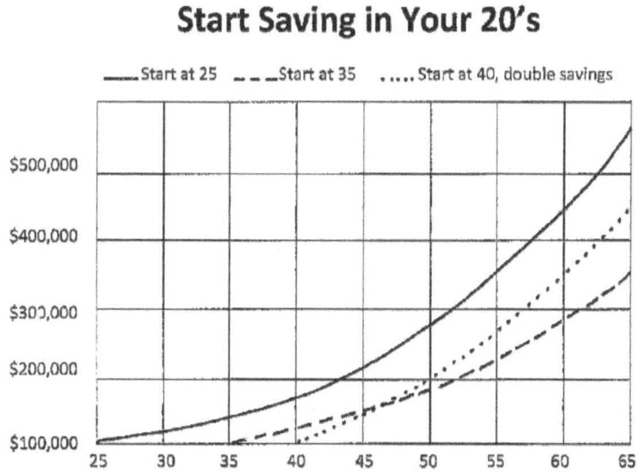

Graph courtesy of Business Insider

Now that you’ve started to save money, how do you protect it?

Protecting your wealth, whatever the amount, is obviously important. The first document you need after you turn 18 is the Advance Heath Directive. Without it, your family or friends will need to go to court to proceed with any and all arrangements. Don't send your family to court.

When my mother died in 2004, I only needed her Advance Health Directive to give instructions to the doctor what should and should not be done for my mom. A will was not required for me to take the right actions on behalf of Mom. I was able to take care of everything having to do with her personal, medical, and end of life care through the Advance Health Directive.

A will gives instructions to the judge. A will is a letter to the Judge that says: "Please judge, I have died, and I want you to make sure that everything I own as assets and property will be given to the people I want my property to go to. My appointed executor will, at your instructions, proceed as I planned while you instruct and preside over."

You usually need a good Estate Attorney to produce documents to make sure you and your family are protected. When you have these documents, your parents, spouse, or partner will be able to act for you without going through the expensive and time - consuming court system to deal with your affairs. This is particularly important as you increase your family. Marriage and children - these are your more precious things -protect them.

Health Insurance

Health Insurance is now part of the Patient Protection and Affordable Care Act (PPACA), sometimes referred to as ACA or Obamacare. Now that insurance is required, this area may be better protected from one of the biggest reasons why people declare bankruptcy: the cost of being ill or having an accident. At the time of this writing, the new administration is trying to repeal the ACA or Obamacare; but so far, there is no good replacement. No matter what happens, you need to have health insurance as we never know when we may need it. Illness has no age, wealth, or discrimination; it can happen to anyone.

Disability Insurance

What if you can't work because of accident or an illness? What are the costs for that versus paying into a program that will protect you? Yeah, at twenty-one some people are bullet proof. But consider Christopher Reeve who played superman, certainly a bullet proof hero. Reeve was an accomplished equestrian. On May 27, 1995, he was thrown off his horse at an equestrian competition in Culpeper, West Virginia. In an instant, he became a quadriplegic. He needed immediate medical care, but more importantly he needed long-term personal care because he was unable to do the five activities of daily living. He needed help in order to have quality of life. No one plans for a life-changing accident, and insurance is the only way to hedge your bets.

Property and Casualty Insurance

When you gain property, you need to think about insurance to protect against losses. Property Casualty offers protection for your car, home, furniture, jewelry, etc. We know we must have car insurance, as most states will take your car registration or driver's license away if not insured, but do you know if your insurance covers someone else? What if a friend borrows your car? Worst case, what if they crash your car? Consider the worst-case scenario, and get yourself covered for that. Once you (or your parents) decide it's time for you to move out of the family home, where do you go?

One thing to consider is proximity to a current job. Do you want to move close to a job, or find a job that close to where you want to live? It's not a trivial question. What do you give up in exchange for a long commute to work? What are the costs in time, gas, car repairs, etc.?

What kind of lifestyle do you want and how does it compare to what you may be planning for the future? You may find a high paying job, but the housing is also high. Does the job lead to a better situation in the future? Will the house appreciate in value? Will the children thrive in a public school or will you need to pay for school as well?

Have you decided how much time you want for you and your family, and where you live - will this be the best place to settle for your future vision and goals?

What about that car? We discussed the dream car. Can you afford it right now? Or is this an expense that you can compromise on? Will a used car with its warranty, affordability, and lower payments leave you with discretionary money to do other things? Will it free up money to invest in retirement and that savings account that will contribute to a new job search?

Budget for Your Dreams

Let's talk about your budget. Track what you're doing now. Start with three or six months of expenses. List everything you buy. Now review the list and find the money. Can you save money by making lunches three times a week and only go out two times? What are your wine or alcohol expenses? How often do you socialize, and what does that cost? It seems draconian at first, but a budget doesn't necessarily suck all the fun out of life. Make healthy lunches and eat them in a park. Hike with family members instead of paying for an expensive amusement park. Meet with friends to play games, or challenge each other to find money saving activities. Make saving a game. Put the money you save aside. Save for short term goals (e.g. that trip, that upgraded car) as well as the long-term goals.

Start Now!

3.

Your Sources of Income

There are different kinds of income. Income is money - cash flow - that pays daily, monthly, and yearly expenses.

Full-Time or Part-Time Jobs

A job is paid position with regular hours. Position, career, profession, trade, work. A task or piece of work. Person with a job has a role in society.

A job is an activity that you get paid for. Most full-time

jobs are for forty or more hours a week. Part-time work is more flexible, but the pay is not as consistent as with full time work. Your employer may pay in different cycles. If you are a child, retired, or disabled, you may be working part time or in a temporary position. Some people work without pay or compensation, in a volunteer position, or as a homemaker. Starting at five years old, children are primarily responsible to learn. Their job is to be a student.

The difference between a job and a career is a career implies higher goals. You still get paid for the work, but maybe you get paid more. Maybe you needed more education to hold your current position. Careers require experience to propel you up to the next level in your field. There is more movement and a higher risk with careers than with a job.

A job can be used to provide funding for college (consider the famous judge James E. Rogan who bartended until he achieved his dream career). Sandra Bullock, Maria Bello, Caroline Pompeo, Dave Matthews, Ellen Degeneres, Jon Stewart, and Bruce Willis all were bartenders before they achieved their dreams of making a living through their art.

A job can provide the income necessary to fulfill your goals, as well teach valuable skills like patience and compassion.

Your Own Business

Do you want to be your own boss? Whether you are a sole proprietor, part of a corporation, or another entity, the goal is to produce income for both you and for your investors, even if those investors are a one-time shot.

Before you launch a business, figure out how much you need to live in addition to the expenses the business will incur. Be very aware that cash is king and that cash flow is the number one thing needed to make a business successful. Most business will fail within 5 years mainly because of cash flow. So, project out what the business cash flow will be for at least six months so that you can make decisions. If the business income statement does not reflect cash and the flow of it in your business, hire a professional to help you make the right moves.

You may be brilliant at inventing the best widget ever, but you may not be brilliant at inventing the best profit and loss (P&L) statement or creating a good strategy and projection of cash flow. A good bookkeeper, Enrolled Agent, or CPA is essential to properly record your business transactions and income.

Interest & Dividends

Interest - usually comes from banks that are FDIC insured and offer Certificates of Deposit also known as CD's or savings accounts that provide income. This interest is usually taxable. Also, be aware of the difference between the interest paid versus inflation or the amount of taxes you will pay. You may actually be risking more income through a simple saving plan than if you put your money in another type of investment.

Dividends_- come from investments, usually stocks or mutual funds, that provide income. Money invested in stocks are not insured through FDIC, nor are they a guaranteed success. It is a distribution from a company's profits and declared by the board of directors.

I provide more information about investment in Strategies of Investment, Chapter 10, p. 97.

Royalties & Rentals

Royalties - are a form of income that use of property a patent, copyright works, franchise, or natural resource. It is compensation for the use of this kind of property.

Rentals - Income from rental property real estate, equipment, party items for events, or intellectual property can all be sources of income. Managing this kind of income may require time and sometimes more expenses. Make sure the income from the rents exceed the expenses.

Social Security

The Social Security Act was signed by Franklin D.

Roosevelt on August 14, 1935. The first taxes were collected January 1937. The benefits started January 1940. When this law was originally passed, it was a retirement plan that only paid the primary worker. Then in 1939 the law was altered to include survivor benefits for spouses and children. By 1956 disability benefits were added. The 1935 Act was a much-needed act; as the first national unemployment compensation, it aided the states in paying for various health and welfare programs while also supporting the Aid to Dependent Children program. Members of Congress, the President, the Vice President, Federal judges, and most political appointees have been paying into this system and have been covered since January 1984.

Age 65 was chosen because it was the starting age in a number of the private pension systems in existence at the time. We had 30 states that had old-age pension systems in operation, 50% used age 65 and 50% used age 70. All your pay is 100% taxed for Social Security. What you may not know is that there is an annual limit for Social Security payments. As of 2017, contribution stops at $127,200 per year. This limit changes each year in the national average wage index.

Social Security is the most common source of retirement income for Americans. According to the Gallup Poll, 88% of retiree's report that they rely on the steady stream of Social Security payments and 55% call Social Security a major source of their retirement income. That being said, this next generation of workers are not as reliant on this system. Just under a third (31%) of current workers think Social Security will be their primary way of paying for retirement, and another 51% of employees are still counting on Social Security, but say it will be a minor source of retirement income.

Many changes in our Social Security system are coming. In order for this resource to continue, it may need to change from what it was in the past to something that supports only those who are considered low income.

The cap for contribution into Social Security may be raised to apply to all earned income instead of the current cap of $127,200. Those who are lucky enough not to need Social Security may simply not receive it. Keep an eye out as Social Security changes develops in our legislation.

Pensions

Just over a third of retirees (38%) (US News) say that traditional pension payments are a significant source of their retirement income. At the time of writing, pensions, as we know them, are being phased out. Instead, companies give their employees the option to start their own retirement savings plans, known as a 401(k). The challenge with this is it places the responsibility of saving for retirement on the employee.

And it's not easy. For instance, the qualified retirement plan must satisfy The Employee Retirement Security Act of 1974 (ERISA) rules, and who knows those off the top of their heads? The reason for phasing out the pension benefit is to take the burden off the employer and pass it on to the employee.

The 401(k) is funded mainly through employee contributions. An employer typically contributes only 2 or 3% to the fund. One of the main areas of concern is most employees do not understand the importance of starting a 401(k) as soon as possible in order to earn a substantial enough lump sum to meet their retirement needs. (See the Ten Mistakes You May Not Know You're Making that reinforces the importance of starting early.)

"The 401(k) is the major source people think they are going to rely on. That's very dangerous because if you are going to rely on it you have to put a lot of money in it," says Frank Newport, editor-in-chief of the Gallup Poll. "Even Americans in their 50s don't have nearly as much in their 401(k) as they would need to retire."

The 403 (b) Plan is a U.S. tax advantage retirement savings available for hospitals staff, public servants, public education organizers, self-employed ministers, and non-profits employees. The employee defers compensation in the plan on a pretax basis.

457 plans are a non-qualified tax advantage plans. This

plan is for governmental and certain non-governmental employees in the United States. The employer provides the plan and the employee defers compensation on a pretax basis.

Gifts

You may have family or trust that distributes gifts annually. The amount allowed in 2017 is $14,000 per person. A gift like this does not need to be from or to family members - anyone can receive this amount. The $14,000 will not be taxed. You do need to understand this includes all gifts given throughout the year. If you received a car for graduation as well as Christmas and birthday gifts and the total exceeded the $14,000, the giver is required to file a Gift Tax Return and the receiver may have to if the giver did not file a gift tax return or has made the agreement for the receiver to file the Gift Tax Return.

Inheritance

While a large inheritance could boost your retirement prospects, it's probably not a good idea to count on receiving one. Since people are living longer and needing more care, it may be possible there will be nothing left to inherit. Many people are expecting to inherit money to help fund retirement and are making no plans to contribute on their own. Gambling that a family member will have not used up all their resources is a bad bet.

Home Equity

Some 18% of retirees are using the equity they have built up in their home to help pay for retirement, perhaps using a reverse mortgage or by significantly downsizing and pocketing the extra cash. Many people believe the sale of their homes will create their retirement income. Or that a reverse mortgage is the solution. But if you do use a reserve mortgage, you or your spouse can never move out of that house. If you do, the debt is due and the home must be sold to pay off the debt. If you sell your home, where are you going to live? If the home is paid for, the only expenses are property taxes and upkeep, a relatively small amount of cash to keep it all going. If you downsize, will you have enough to take care of you plus pay rent? What is the rent cost? Will you like where you are moving?

Before jumping into a reverse mortgage or selling then renting, resist the promises and check it out first. Make sure you understand the economic and social consequences of your actions. Hire a Certified Financial Planner and avoid mistakes.

Annuities

Annuities is a contract between the insurance company and you in which you give a lump sum or payments to give you a study stream of income. There are different kinds of annuities, for this chapter; however, we are only looking at the immediate annuity that allows you to get a stream of income very much like a pension. An annuity insurance product may or may not be right for you. This may have riders that guarantee the amount you will be receiving. Be aware that every benefit has a cost and this may be too costly. It truly depends on each person and the strategies and structure of their income. More information can be found under the Strategies for Investing.

Starting a Business

Like when you take a trip or buy a car, you need a plan. Starting a business is no different. Making important key financial decisions, looking at the legal and tax aspects of what you want to do, and managing your next steps are crucial to success. Remember Benjamin Franklin, the father of time management once said, "Failing to plan is planning to fail." About 50% of all businesses survive for five years or more (USA Today). Do you want to survive? Even thrive? Then you need to consider these ten steps:

1: Write a business plan

2: Get business training and advice

3: location (location is crucial to your success)

4: Finance your business

5: Decide on the legal and tax structure (this will also determine your IRS ID)

6: File with the IRS, the State you want to do business in and register the business name. Pay attention how you are ("Doing Business As or DBA) If you name your business and then you decide to shorten the name or use a second name by using the name of your city, county be careful to make sure you follow the law for DBA.

7: Register with state and local tax authorities, workers' compensation, unemployment, and disability insurance.

8: Obtain the required business licenses and permits (get a list of federal, state, and local licenses and permits). Contact your city, county, or state governments.

9: You as the Employer are responsible to take the legal steps for hiring employees.

10: Find free training and professional coaches (local assistance is available through SBA offices, Chamber of Commerce).

Some of the initial issues to consider are: copyrights, trademarks, patents, and a marketing plan.

Work with someone who, ideally, has a passion for what you are doing and who also has a firm grasp on what you are trying to accomplish. Have another team member (or the same one if you are lucky,) be devoted to keeping you from making avoidable mistakes. As a CFP® and a tax expert, I help avoid mistakes that cause business failure.

Resources for Startups

You can find information through the Small Business Administration (SBA) on environmentally-friendly, home-based, online, minority-owned, veteran-owned, and woman-owned businesses.

One of the best places to start is the SBA Small Business Administration website www.sba.gov. They offer a plethora of information, and you can also contact them and work with a mentor by speaking to someone in your local area SCORE. The SCORE Association is a nonprofit association of volunteer business counselors that have retired from very successful businesses and now want to help others. They are trained to counsel, advise, and mentor aspiring entrepreneurs and business owners. Contact your local SCORE Association sponsored by SBA. You can email them or visit their local offices and make an appointment; they also have online workshops, and you can sign up for E-newsletters.

4.

Jobs - Livelihood - Occupation

Jobs and Benefits

While staring a business may be exciting, sometimes steady work is more important, and better fits your current needs. Like benefits. Employers may offer optional benefits that include different programs for employees, such as:

Health Care Insurance

Disability Insurance

Life Insurance

Retirement / Pension Plans

Flexible Compensation

Paid Leave

Profit Sharing/Stock Options

(the list is pretty standard – for more information, check out www.Money-zine.com)

When negotiating for a job, remember all of the above benefits. Also, you can ask for an early salary review if your starting pay is low, and you still want the job. An earlier performance and salary review is an easy way to salvage a low starting offer. Just remember that most employers review salaries yearly. Six- and nine-month reviews are the most typical, though you might be able to ask for a three-month review.

However, asking for an early salary review on a salary that both you and your hiring manager know is inflated will make you look arrogant and greedy, so exercise caution when deciding to do so.

Consider negotiating for better workplace equipment and software. This is an often-forgotten question. Ask what types of office equipment is standard, what operating systems the devices run on, what programs are regularly installed, and how that equipment is supported. These are very astute questions to ask in today's working world. Accessibility to certain equipment and software could be especially crucial for employees who will need to travel frequently. Depending on the job you're seeking, you might want to find out about these devices during the interview process and not when renegotiating at a later date.

Remember asking for a company cellphone because you're expected to be on call is within reason, but asking for an iPhone with an unlimited data plan could be pushing it, particularly for an entry-level employee. Many companies offer laptops, phones, and tablets for certain employees. But asking for a specific type of phone or tablet, or saying that you only use Apple products could come off as snobbish and could potentially kill your job offer.

Flex-time and telecommuting may be options you can consider. Asking a manager for a non-traditional work schedule is not uncommon. Ask about the telecommuting policies.

Before you open your mouth to utter the phrase "summer Fridays" during negotiations, find out how the company's current employees rate their corporate culture and work-life balance. It's unlikely that you'll receive a special compensation as a new employee that none of the existing employees have.

An employee expense allowance may be possible provided that the company is willing to reimburse you for money spent while traveling for work or when completing assignments. It certainly won't hurt your chances to make inquiries about this is if you're weighing a job offer that requires extensive travel. Remember that for certain professions, work-travel expenses include gas mileage, frequent flier miles, and even corporate credit card access, and are therefore up for discussion.

There's also room for employees to negotiate receiving an allowance for on-site parking fees or public transportation. Note you should research this and other opportunities before asking for any of these less-than-standard benefits. It is important to know about the company and its culture. You don't want to make any request that's going to end up counterproductive.

You should definitely ask about bonuses, stock options, and shares if you're seeking employment in the private sector. Just look for what's the standard to receive in each industry, and do some research into what's customary with the particular employer you're interviewing with.

You should also stay abreast of the corporate health of the company where you're seeking employment. You can do this by setting up a Google Alert, which notifies you when articles on your business or industry are published. Read the information under the "About Us" link on the corporate website, and using corporate research sites like www.Hoovers.com.

Professional development courses may be available. These are opportunities the company provides for advancement, obtaining certifications, and additional development.

Remember that the occasional class fee is different from tuition reimbursement; the latter you probably can't negotiate. Employers either provide tuition reimbursement or they don’t. It may be worth mentioning that tuition reimbursement provides a tax credit for the company. Remember it is very unlikely that you will be able to get a company to reimburse you for education that isn't related to your career.

5.

Instant Wealth - Windfall

You have just received a windfall, and you do not know what to do. Or maybe you have a list of things you want to do and are ready to spend that money starting tomorrow.

Hold on, not quite yet. First, let's define instant wealth. Instant wealth is receiving a large sum of money, larger than what you are accustomed to. That amount can range from $5,000 to millions; it's a relative amount. What isn't relative is that more often than not, when we are lucky enough to receive instant wealth, we often have no idea how to handle it.

There are too many stories about lottery winners who

get it all, then just as quickly lose everything plus more, falling from rich to well below the poverty line.

Sharon Tirabassi won ten million dollars in the Ontario Lottery. Ten years later, she has nothing to show for it. She spent almost all her winnings on a big house, fancy cars, designer clothes, lavish parties, exotic trips, handouts to family, and loans to friends. Today she works part time, rides the bus, and lives in a rental house. What remains is in trust for her six children; the money will become available when they turn 26. Her warning to the newly rich: "If you're not disciplined, you'll go broke. I don't care how much money you have."

Other well-documented examples are celebrities and athletes who earned enormous amounts of cash for years only to end up with nothing, not even their health. It can also be said that money will not protect you from bad choices.

"Iron Mike" Tyson won 19 professional fights by knockout. He became the heavy weight champion of the world. In 1992, he was convicted of sexual assault and served three years in prison. When he got out, no amount of comeback matches could get him back his mojo, and after biting off a piece of Evander Holyfield's ear during a 1997 fight, Tyson was disqualified. He never again won another championship.

Tyson had won over $400 million in his boxing career, so money shouldn't have been a problem. However, he spent almost all his earnings in extravagant living. His divorce settlement was for $9 million, and he ended up owing $13 million to the IRS. He filed for bankruptcy in 2003 claiming debts of $27 million.

Michael Vick played for the Atlanta Falcons and had signed a record $62 million six-year contract, along with a $3 million signing bonus. Three years later, he signed a ten-year extension worth $130 million, making him the highest-paid player in the NFL. In 2007, Michael Vick went to prison for running an illegal interstate dog fighting ring. The prison sentence kept him from playing for almost two years. He lost his NFL salary and all his endorsements including a very lucrative Nike sponsorship. The loss of income and bad financial management forced him to declare bankruptcy while still in federal prison.

Kenny Anderson earned an estimated $60 million during his NBA career after playing for nine different teams. He was married three times. Tami Akbar, his first wife, was able to challenge their prenuptial agreement and received half his assets and $8,500 a month in child support. Anderson had six other children and two other ex-wives he was supporting. He was making monthly payments on his mother's house. He also owned eight cars and an estate in Beverly Hills. He gave himself a $10,000-a-month allowance that he referred to as "hanging out money." At the time of his bankruptcy filing, his monthly expenses totaled $41,000.

These athletes all worked hard and sacrificed many things to make it to the top of their professions. But, when it came to finances, they made spectacularly bad decisions. They were unable to exercise the discipline it takes to manage that kind of instant wealth.

You don't need to be a pro-athlete to come into instant wealth. It most commonly comes to us through inheritance. According to CNBC, which is a casual reference at best, "In the next few decades, some $30 trillion will be transferred from one generation to the next." This transfer has already begun as the War Babies and other generations have gone.

We know that some of you have been introduced to wealth while others have not. We do not yet know how the next generation will handle their instant wealth. What we do know is you need to prepare now in order to make good decisions later. Find the right certified advisors, financial planners, attorneys, therapists, enrolled agents, and/or CPAs now; don't wait for a crisis (a good crisis, but a crisis nonetheless).

Stock options from your employer can also make you instantly rich. The way this wealth is transferred and handled is yet another question a professional can best answer. If you are eligible for stock options or if stock is part of your compensation package, find out what that means exactly. Again, good news can quickly turn into a major headache if you are unprepared.

Divorce settlements can also be counted as instant wealth. Prepare to take this extra money into account and plan how you are going to make this money last. Is paying off debt the right thing to do or should you invest and use the resulting income to pay down debt. Have you received half the business as part of the settlement? Is it time to make sure your family is protected do you need to take care of risk either through self-insurance, insurance, or special trust and other contracts that protect your assets.

Inheritance is instant wealth, you need to stop and check and see how the assets will transfer. Will this be taxable? Will it be distributed in single lump sum, or will it trickle in? Will it be property that is transferred to you? How will this be managed, do you need professionals like a CFP®, CPA or Attorneys? Did you inherit life insurance, an IRA or retirement plans as a beneficiary. Did you inherit investments, antiques, heirloom's, land or other personal and tangible property? Did you end up with the family business?

Are you taking your retirement in a lump sum? That too is instant wealth. You'll need to invest and plan if you want that money to last until you are in your nineties.

These are all resources that need to be harnessed and protected. When it comes to instant wealth, the most important response is discipline. Planning your lifestyle and monitoring your investments need to be considered. Find certified financial planners, attorneys, and therapists who will help you not only grow but protect your assets from the risk of your emotional roller coaster. Hire professionals, and for a time, you may want to keep your windfall to yourself. Don't give friends and family the opportunity to take advantage of you.

6.

Credit and Debt

So how much debt should I have? Good question. Before you start acquiring debt, you should figure this out. Use this equation to find your debt-to-income ratios:

total debt ÷ income X 100 =% of debt.

You can also use a calculator found on the internet to calculate when you will become debt free. A good website to use is: http://money.cnn.com/calculator/pf/debt-free/.

Before you think of buying a car, getting a credit card or accruing debt, figure out the amount of debt you can afford before you borrow. Income X % of good credit 36% = the amount you can borrow with your current income. 36% represents the amount of credit you can afford with your income. This is good credit and a good way to start without getting into financial trouble with too much debt and not able to repay causing bad credit and financial hardship.

If you have no credit score or very low one you can establish credit or rebuild credit by getting a credit card that is backed with a deposit. The credit is the amount on deposit you must pay every month on time to show proof you are able to make payments and pay back thus establishing credit. Most banks, credit union or credit card companies will issue this kind of credit card.

Before you purchase an item with debt, ask yourself do you need it or want it? There is a difference.

Debt-to-Income Ratio Worksheet

Your debt-to-income ratio indicates how much of your income goes toward debt payments and can be used to figure out whether or not you have too much debt.

Monthly payments (A)

Mortgage	$_______________
Minimum credit card payment	$_______________
Car loan	$_______________
Student loans	$_______________
Alimony/child support payments	$_______________
Other loans/debt	$_______________
Total (A):	$_______________

Monthly Income (B)

Income from wages	$_______________
Alimony/child support	$_______________
Bonuses or Overtime	$_______________
Other Income	$_______________
Total (B):	$_______________

Debt to Income Ratio = A ÷ B x 100 = %

Your results: _________________

36% or less - Good debt amount, avoid incurring more debt .

37% - 42% - Not bad, start reducing your debt to get better loan rates.

50%-plus - A dangerous situation, start paying off these debts, now, not tomorrow. You may want to consider professional help.

Good Debt

Is there "good debt"? Some of your debt might be considered an investment.

"How can anything as bad as debt be considered an investment?" If you incur debt to purchase an item that over time increases in value, that is considered good debt.

Let's look at the traditional example of good debt: a home purchase. A home usually appreciates in value after three to five years. ("Five-year Rule" generally accepted throughout the investment world.) The mortgage loan you take out to pay for your home is an investment. Student loans can also be a good debt as it's an investment in your future. A college education will provide you with higher earning potential over the long term. The key is to use that education and degree as leverage to make more money than you would have without them. This good debt pays for itself over time and contributes to your future.

Bad Debt

What is the negative to this equation? There is good debt, and there is bad. Bad debt is paying for something later so you can have it today. Wimpy often said to Popeye, "I'll gladly pay you Tuesday for a hamburger today." This is a great example of bad debt. A hamburger does not increase in value; it is consumed. This kind of debt creates an unhealthy financial situation: owing money for something that is gone. Credit card debt is often considered bad debt, so use credit cards wisely.

You should never accumulate debt to purchase everyday items like clothes or food. If you use a credit card for these types of purchases, you should pay the balance in full each month.

Debt used to finance a vacation is another type of bad debt. Even though it might help you feel better and be more productive once you return, a vacation does not appreciate in value over time. It is a good idea to plan how you will pay for the vacation even before boarding the plane. If you do use a credit card, plan to pay it off as soon as possible. If you can't pay off the vacation within the month, consider another less expensive way to relax.

Practice Debt Control

You acquire good debt by making wise decisions about your future. Don't acquire debt just to have good debt. You may make the decision to obtain your master's degree to increase your earning potential. Good debt is that student loan. Before you take on the loan, make sure you have a plan for how you are going to pay it back.

Ok, you have debt, and you're analyzing your financial picture; you are trying to decide what is the best debt to pay off. Usually, focus on paying off your bad debts first. Bad debt provides no value, plus they cost more due to higher interest. Because there is no collateral, the credit companies take all the risk. Credit cards and other unsecured debt should be the first to be retired. After those are cleared, tackle the mortgage or student loan.

Some people consider using good debt to pay off bad debt, like getting a mortgage for $110,000 instead of $100,000 and using the extra to pay off credit card balances. This isn't a good idea for several reasons. First, repaying debt with debt is never a good idea. Second, it ends up taking longer to pay off the mortgage than it would have otherwise. Third, the higher mortgage increases your monthly payments and the time it takes to build equity in your home. Use cash to repay debts, not more debt.

You must still be careful that you don't take on too much debt, even if it's good debt.

Bad Debt Categories - 5 Things Not Worth Acquiring Debt Over

1. Going on a destination vacation.

2. Buying designer purses/shades/shoes/you-name-it.

3. Paying off other debt (unless you're doing a balance transfer or debt consolidation loan with better terms).

4. Buying gifts for others.

5. Getting furniture for the new house.

None of these are things that appreciate in value. So, once they are in your hands, it's over. And the debt keeps mounting long after the purchase thrill is gone.

In fact, all of these depreciate soon after you use them. You're often left with debt and nothing to show for it. Instead of using credit cards or loans to pay for consumable goods, save up and use cash. That way you enjoy your purchase without worrying about paying for it later.

Good Debt Can Go Bad

If you're not careful, that good debt you took out can

turn bad. Don't take out more debt than you need to. Take out just enough student loans to cover your education expenses, just enough mortgage to purchase your home, and just enough business loans to cover your startup costs.

Make your payments on time or, if you can’t, contact your lender ASAP. The key is making timely loan payments which will keep your credit score intact. All it takes is a couple months of late payments to reduce your credit score and wreck your credit. So never miss a payment - it doesn’t matter if the debt is good or bad.

7.
The Seven Drainers of Wealth

1. Inflation

What in the world is inflation? Merriam-Webster's dictionary states that inflation is "a continuing rise in the general price level usually attributed to an increase in the volume of money and credit relative to available goods and services".

Inflation looks and feels like the price of something I bought last year cost more to buy this year.

For example, a postage stamp in 2001 cost 34 cents. In 2017, it cost 49 cents. Same letter, same destination, higher price. In 2001 the average price of a gallon of milk was $1.19, and in 2017 the price of a gallon of milk was $4.50. The difference of 15 cents for the stamp and $3.31 cents for the milk is inflation - the rise of the cost of living between 2001 and 2017. This is a risk that needs to be calculated when saving as inflation is one of the biggest eaters of our earnings and wealth. Inflation is one of the reasons a cost of living increase in pay is so important. If we are lucky, the cost of living increase will keep pace with the rate of inflation. We all hope it at least meets the 2 or 3% average increase a year. So, if you are making an average salary of $50,000 per year and your earnings increases at 2%, the amount of increase is $1000 a year. We divide this by 52 weeks. The increase now is $19.23 per week. It may not be big dollars, but you are at least staying even with inflation.

In light of inflation, $100,000 in a CD paying 1.25% is losing you money. If inflation is 2%, you are losing 0.75%.

2. Taxes

Taxes are the second biggest eater of our wealth. The government wants their revenue from your earnings whether wages, business, rental, or interest and dividends. What you pay depends on your tax bracket and the state in which you live. The Tax Code has 73,954 pages of tax law we must all abide by to live in the USA.

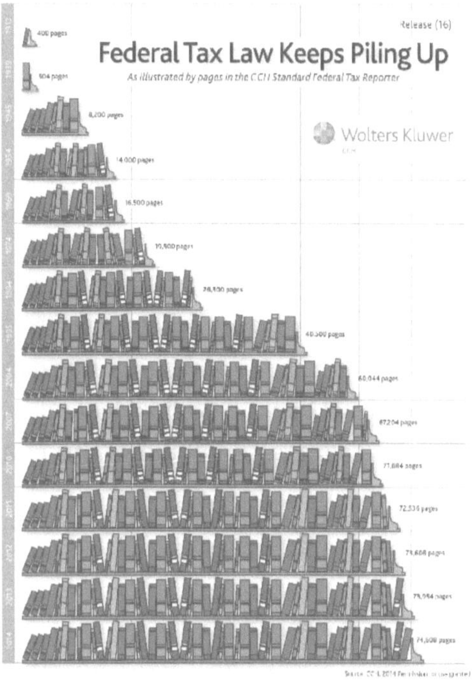

Taxes include sales, car registration, property, etc. When these go up, you are keeping less of your income. Let's take the $100,000 you are saving in a CD. This year you have lost 0.75% to inflation, and the bank is paying you 1.25% interest. $1250 interest - $750 inflation = $500 earned. But wait, you must pay taxes on that $1250 interest earned. Let's assume you are in the 20% federal tax bracket and your state tax is 3%. That makes $1250 x 23% = $287.50. After inflation, you earned $500 minus $287. 50 for taxes leaving you $212.50. Good reasons to watch for taxes and inflation. Take time to see your tax specialist, an Enrolled Agent, or CPA before the end of the year. October is a good month for a financial checkup.

3. Debt

According to Merriam-Webster, "debt" comes from the Latin word "debitum," meaning "something owed."

Debt is something owed to one party or person and is under a contract that spells out what you owe, the cost of borrowing, the payments, when will this debt go default, how to pay it back, date this debt matures and must be paid off, and how to get out of this contract.

A debt can also be a moral or ethical obligation. Not all debt is financial.

4. Interest

This is the cost of borrowing money, and it is usually charged by the company or persons you borrowed the money from. This is usually calculated as percentage of the principal owed to the creditor per year. When someone asks, "What is the percentage of interest you are paying?" - that is the interest rate the creditor wants from you to borrow their money.

There are many ways interest is calculated: 360 days or 365 days a year is called the day count convention. The standard convention is the Annual Percentage Convention, or APR for short. This is widely used and is required in the United States and United Kingdom by regulation.

You will find that interest rates may be fixed or variable (also known as floating rate or adjustable). In variable rate loans, the interest that you pay for borrowing is tied to a benchmark such as LIBOR (London Interbank Offered Rate) or, in the case of inflation-indexed bonds, connected to the inflation rate.

When loans are less than the principal sum, the debtor (or borrower) may have to pay points or upfront fees charged for the cost of borrowing the money. There may be an additional principal due at the end of the term. This is the same as an increase in interest. This is sometimes referred to as banker's dozen, a play on "baker's dozen" - owe twelve (a dozen), receive a loan of eleven (a banker's dozen). Note: the effective interest rate is not equal to the discount; if one borrows $10 and must repay $11, then this is ($11 - $10)/$10 = 10% interest; however, if one borrows $9 and must repay $10, then this is ($10 - $9)/$9 = 11.11% interest.

Repayment

Payment can be made in three main ways. 1. You can pay back the full amount of your debt at maturity of your loan. 2. The principal loan can be amortized so that you can make weekly, monthly, or annual payments for the term of the loan. 3. You can have a partial payment plan. For example, 5 years of payment at one rate, then a balloon payment is due. A balloon payment is when the whole loan is due and must be paid unless refinanced. It depends what kind of loan you have agreed to. Not a bad idea to talk to a CFP about your loan and the terms before you sign.

Collateral and Recourse

Collateral (or recourse) means that your debt is attached to something that can be repossessed: a car, motorcycle, home, etc. Collateral may be your tax refund (in the case of a government), specific assets (in the case of a company), or a home (in the case of a consumer). Unsecured debt is a financial obligation for which creditors do not have recourse to your assets to satisfy their claims. If you decide not to pay back your loan, you now have forgiveness of debt called COD (Cancellation of Debt). The debt cancellation amount is reported income and is taxable as ordinary income. Make sure you talk to your Enrolled Agent or CPA about the tax consequence of making this kind of deal.

Types of Borrowers

Individual

Most individuals have a mortgage loan, car loan, and credit cards debts. For most families, this is the way to get their Wimpy hamburger today and pay for it on

Tuesday. The idea of individual debt is you will pay back the loan with future money. This kind of debt helps individuals purchase now before they've earned the money to pay.

Borrowing before you have earned the money and using credit cards instead of cash can lead to being unaware of your spending which then can lead to over spending. This could lead to being unable to pay back the "loan." You also may view this kind of purchase as monopoly money, often credit cards don't represent "real" money until it's too late and the bill arrives. You may wonder, at the end of the month, what the heck you bought. A good rule of thumb to ask before any purchase: do you want it or need it? If you want it and can pay it off at the end of month, good. If you want it and you cannot pay for it by the end of the month, don't buy it. Remember that needs and wants are hard to untangle. It's worth the effort.

Be careful about borrowing from friends and family. Do you intend to quickly pay the money back? Does the cost of borrowing the money include how it will affect your relationship? How important is this relationship compared to the item you wish to buy? Is this a need or a want?

Businesses

Companies may have different kinds of financing for operations or raising capital.

Corporate debt can be formed by a term loan. Usually it is an agreement for a fixed amount of money and for a specific amount of time. The loan, as a commercial loan interest, is calculated as a percentage of the principal per year. This interest is to be paid by that date, or may be paid periodically in the interval, such as annually or monthly.

There are syndicated loans, and a company may also issue bonds. Bonds have a fixed lifetime, usually figured in years. A bond with a 30-year life is a long-term bond. A bond is a promise to pay back the money that the company borrowed from the investor with a promise to pay interest or dividends for the use of the investors' money.

A company can also use a Letter of Credit, or LC. A Letter of Credit can be used for exporting and importing, land development, as well as a bill of lading.

Many companies will use debt to leverage the investment in their assets. Leveraging is the return on the equity. The leverage needs to be a proportion of debt to equity. This is extremely important as it determines the riskiness of the investment.

Governments

Governments issue debt to pay for ongoing expenses as well as major capital projects. Government debt may be issued by sovereign states as well as by local governments, sometimes known as municipalities.

US Treasury Bonds and or Muni Bonds.

Default

Every type of debtors will default on debt from time to time, with various cost and penalties depending on the terms of the debt and the law governing default in the relevant jurisdiction. When a borrower is classified as risky, they must pay higher interest to compensate for the higher risk of defaulting on the loan. Usually the lender will assess the risk of default and charge appropriately for the risk taken. One-way risk is assessed is through credit scores. A high credit score means a lower risk to the lender. That's why high credit scores help you obtain lower interest rates; you're a less of a risk.

Individuals and companies may go into bankruptcy if they are unable to satisfy their debts. Traditions in some cultures demand that this be done on a regular (often annual) basis, in order to prevent systemic discriminations between groups in society or to prevent anyone becoming a specialist in holding debt and coercing repayment. See Jubilee year, Leviticus, Lev 25:10 in the Bible.

According to English Law, deceiving a creditor into relinquishing the debt is criminal under Theft Act 1978.

5. Health Cost

The health cost continues to grow as our national health expenditures will hit $3.35 trillion in 2017; this works out to be about $10,345 for every person and child in the US. There is an annual increase of 4.8%. In actuality, this is an average and not everyone spends this much on health. There is about 5% of the population that are frail or ill will need this kind much care. We have to be prepared to pay for health insurance and also be able to pay for drugs. $10,345 works out to about $862 a month, and we are talking about basic, not extraordinary, care.

6. Living Too Long

The good news is that we're living longer lives. The bad news? That generally translates into a longer period of time that you'll be dependent on your retirement income, and a higher risk that you may out live your income and assets.

Life expectancy has increased at a steady pace over the years and is expected to continue increasing. According to the U.S. Census Bureau, by 2030 1 in 5 Americans will be 65 or older, which translates into 72 million people. (U.S. Census Bureau, 65+ in the United States: 2005). According to the National Center for Health Statistics, the average 65-year-old American can expect to live for another 19.1 years.

For many of us, it's not unreasonable to plan for a retirement that lasts for 25 years or more, which means your income and savings will need to last that long as well. When you create your Financial Plan, make sure your CFP® has made these calculations and has advised you what you need to do to accomplish and take care of your long, beautiful life.

7. Living Without Purpose & Not Passing Along Family Values

So, what does it all mean? Living without purpose creates wanderers and wasters. Without meaning, it's difficult to discover solid ground. Time goes by so fast that it can be easy to miss your opportunity to find the special purpose of your life. Ideally every day is one of discovery and adventure. Your goal should be to wake up with joy.

Everyone has a definition of success. Success can be about money or things. However, without purpose there is no meaning. Achieve clarity about your purpose, and you'll be rewarded with a wonderful outlook on your life. When you find your purpose, you'll feel good about who you are, what you stand for, and where you're heading. A peace will come into your life and replace the emptiness. You will also be happier, more motivated, and self-assured - a person with a mission. Something will happen to your soul and inner peace. As Robert Byrne once said, "The purpose of life is a life of purpose."

According to the Merriam-Webster Dictionary, family values "especially of a traditional or conservative kind … are held to promote the sound functioning of the family and to strengthen the fabric of society." Some of the words that explain what family values the past and future generations will embrace: honesty, love, responsibility, sacrifice, forgiveness, belonging, communication, respect, and generosity.

8.

Ten Mistakes You May Not Know You're Making

We have our goals and our dreams, but are we sabotaging them before we even make our first steps?

These are the mistakes I see most often in my practice. They are easy to make, easy to overlook, and yes, easy to remedy.

1. Not Planning

Benjamin Franklin said: "If you fail to plan, you are planning to fail!" Failure to plan appears time and time again.

Contrary to what you may think, planning actually helps with change. When we fail to plan, we are not ready to make changes or prepared to anticipate change. When a big change smacks us in the face, it often takes up to three to four months to finally react and really understand what has happened.

Without a strategy, you have no information to help you make future decisions when something goes wrong. What is the new plan, when was the last time you reviewed it, and does this still make sense? Are you still going in the right direction?

2. No 401k, 403 b, 457, Sep, or IRA Savings

Without a retirement plan, you will have no income if you are unable to work. If you are self-employed or working for a company that does not provide a pension, you could lose 100% of your income.

Social Security, Pension Benefits, and extra medical expenses are uncertain, and you need to take responsibility for your own future. This is known as the three-legged stool effect. As you know, a stool needs three legs for it to stand: leg one in retirement is Pension, leg two is Personal Savings (401k, 403b, 457, IRA, SEP, SIMPLE IRA), and leg three is Social Security. If your company does not provide a pension, you lose one of the legs, and you need to replace it with life insurance, an annuity, an alternative investment, or another form of asset producing income.

3. No Insurance

Not purchasing or having insurance risks your family, business, and property. Lack of insurance puts you at risk for a major loss risking huge dollars for pennies. The huge dollars are what you insure: your car, home, life, and family. The pennies are the premium you will pay monthly, quarterly, or annually. Talk to your CFP®, and see what can be done to protect your large assets.

4. Spending retirement funds before you retire

Your retirement takes a long time both to establish and to grow. Don't use retirement funds for any expense except retirement. It's tempting but do not use it for establishing a business, college, or personal use.

Because time and yield are important to create wealth, when you take out money from your retirement and you have not reached 59 ½, you are paying not only federal (and sometimes state) income taxes but you are also paying penalties of 10% (plus 3-4% depending on state taxes). This can total between 41% and 53% tax. That loss can never be recuperated, you will have no time to make this up, and the risk to get a higher return is too great.

For example, if you take $20,000 out, you will add this to your income raising your income an additional $20,000 and your income tax. Let's say your regular tax is 27% including state taxes, then add 14% penalties and that will make your tax 41% of what you took out: $20,000 X 41% = $8,200. You can see you now instead of having $20,000, you actually have $11,800 to use, and this just gets bigger with more taxes owed because you will need to take out more than $20,000 in order to have $20,000 to use and pay taxes. Not a good idea.

This is your future income. Do not touch, only invest, contribute and deposit at the maximum that is available for you. Every year increase your distribution if you can; it will increase your future yield. Find a CFP® that is willing to help you move forward with this plan.

5. Buying a business for a family member

Of course, you want to help family. But even if you have done all your due diligence and it all looks good, it still may not turn out well. Remember that unless losing all the money you invest won't make a difference and you are prepared to fund this effort for at least five years, it is a project best avoided. Because often there will be no way of recovering this investment.

Case Study:

The Johnson's decided to purchase a business for their daughter Mary. After doing all the due diligence -

looking at the sales tax reports and tax returns, and checking the industry - they felt they had done everything to make sure the business was solid.

They figured that the $200,000 they were putting up for the business was like investing in a college degree. In addition, when the business started making money, it would take care of itself and provide a solid career for their daughter.

The business did not make any money. From November 2006 to 2010, the losses ended up being $125,000 per year. The total investment was around $550,000; finally, the Johnson's had no more capital to add to the business. In February of 2010, they got in touch with a broker to put the business on the market. The asking price was $80,000 which would take care of all the outstanding bills. The broker did inform the parents that because of the crash, it may take a long time to get that amount.

After a few months of attempting to sell while offering 50-70% store wide discounts in an effort to stay open, there were still no offers. Finally, in April, an offer was made for $25,000. The family worked the numbers and after payroll, taxes, broker commission, and some other expenses, they countered with $32,000. They sold the business for $32,000. The sale price did not even cover all the expenses. They were not able to sell for the full amount; they just wanted to stop the bleeding. Even after the sale, there was still $50,000 of back rent and expenses to settle, and a loan of $155,000.

They also sued the original owner, a Mr. Kahn, for $88,000 for non-disclosure. They won the suit but winning doesn't mean you can collect. They then had to hire a detective to find the money. They placed a 10-year lien against the seller, but unfortunately Mr. Kahn had left the country.

If there are no assets or you do not have information to collect on a bad debt, you are out of luck and money. The lesson here is you know what you know, you know what you think you know, and you don't know what you don't know.

6. Paying off short term debt with your mortgage

Short-term debt for a business is defined as any financial obligations that are due within a 12-month period. For the individual, short-term debt is often credit cards. By putting this debt in a 30-year loan, you are now paying more than double for this property. How do you buy a new car after you put $29,000 or more into your mortgage and your car now needs replacing you have not paid off the car you financed into your mortgage? Not a very good idea. Or racking up charges on a credit card with no plan to pay down or stop charging. You are only adding more and more debt that increasingly becomes more expensive to maintain. This becomes a vicious circle with no end.

7. Doing it yourself - DIY

I have a friend who started a wonderful business. He was an excellent sales man but a terrible accountant. Additionally, because he did not seek out a good contract attorney to set up his business correctly my friend ended up losing everything. Getting a business attorney to review your contracts is a must.

You would not remove your own appendix, so don't go cheap when hiring necessary expertise. Don't go to Legal Zoom or an online DIY, like a ROBO advisor. You, your investments, and your business, are worth good service and quality advice.

Make sure your people are properly licensed, insured and bonded. It is not difficult to check people out and make sure they possess at least this minimum of requirements. State boards and contractor's licenses, FINRA, State Insurance licenses, State legal Bar, and BBB Better Business Bureau for some and there is many more. Check the people you are going to work with. Professionals expect you to check, we'd be disappointed if you didn't.

8. Rental property & Equipment

Instead of buying, you can rent most things: Equipment, commercial buildings, single family homes, Auto, trailer, Recreational Vehicle RV, and event items like tent, glasses, dinner settings, table chairs etc.

For instance, let's check out and see if renting a RV is a better deal than buying. When you buy your own RV, that means maintenance. Before buying anything large: RV, boat, car, house, make sure you understand the maintenance costs.

Friends of mine decided they wanted a RV. Sometimes these are emotional purchases, and in this case, it was. They really did not investigate the additional costs of maintenance. They soon found out that a flat tire could not be changed or replaced like a car. Nope. They had to call out for a special truck to change the tire. This cost them extra for the vehicle trip, the tire and the lost time waiting for the RV Tire Specialist. Consider some of these additional costs before you buy.

How often will you use this piece of property: once a week, monthly or maybe twice a year to go camping? Compare the cost of this RV against how much you will use it. What is the resale value? What about buyers? It is not easy to sell a used RV as my friend found out. They never got their money back for the use of the RV. Had they run all the numbers, including how much they would drive the RV, where they would drive it and how many times, they may have decided to just rent. And that would have saved them both money and time.

9. Rent or Buy Home

Home ownership is considered and integral part of the American Dream. The question to ask, is it your dream?

Many people think buying a house is better than renting because home owners get a tax advantage over renters. Is this a good enough reason? The answer is no. Buying a house just because of the tax write off is not a good reason to buy your own home.

A good reason to buy a home is assure no one will ever ask you to leave. You want to hang pictures. You want to poke holes into the walls, you want to remove a wall. You want to do what you want without needing to ask permission.

You'll know you are ready to buy because you'll be able to afford good property insurance to protect your investment.

You are ready to buy a home because you are OK with the maintenance costs, like painting inside and outside, new carpets or floors, new roof and gutters and a million things that will come up in the course of staying in this large purchase. If you have decided you can take this responsibility, then the tax write- off for your interest paid to the Mortgage Company and your property tax, is a great bonus, but not a good reason to buy.

10. No will, trust or Advance Health Care Directive

It is very important to protect your family by having a will, a trust, and an Advance Health Care Directive. Without these important documents, you are leaving a mess that is costly, will cause conflicts, may cause your family additional grief, and potentially result in the wrong people controlling your assets.

Everyone 18 or older needs a Health Care Directive to make sure they are taken care of in the manner they wish. Don't leave critical decisions to a doctor or even to next of kin. An Advance Health Care Directive controls what happens to you when you cannot make decisions yourself. It will give the person you have appointed directions, and you will have been a part of directing this person.

If you die, the Advance Healthcare Directive will take care of your funeral and your remains according to your wishes, not those of the state or anyone else.

The Advance Health Care Directives for each state are available online or at the hospital in your community. You can also get this document through your health insurance. Kaiser Permanente has one online. You just need to print it out, answer the questions, and have it witnessed or notarized.

I strongly recommend that you do this. It will take about an hour, and you will need to have it notarized or two people must witness your signature. Please check your state website online and your local hospital for this document.

You should give a copy to your doctor, your dentist, the

hospital, and the persons appointed, and you should also have one available for the fire department paramedics when they come to your home to help you in an emergency.

9.

Divorce - dissolution of Marriage

Starting Over

If you and your spouse are going through a divorce or considering a divorce, it is important to adequately plan for the financial changes that are coming. It is all too easy to be blindsided by the unexpected costs of dividing a household.

A divorce attorney may be able to help with the division of property and the establishment of support payments, but their financial expertise only goes so far.

Certified Divorce Financial Analyst® (CDFA®) consultants specialize in helping families adjust to the financial changes associated with divorce.

No Fault Divorce

In 1970, California was the first State to pass the "No Fault Divorce." Other No-Fault states are Wisconsin, Washington, Oregon, Nevada, Nebraska, Montana, Missouri, Minnesota, Michigan, Kentucky, Kansas, Iowa, Indiana, Hawaii, Florida, Colorado and the District of Columbia. The other 33 states allow for no fault however, they do have the option of using fault to claim divorce like adultery, abandonment, or cruelty. Note that divorce is a state and county issue.

To file, you need to file in the state or county of your primary residence. In a No-Fault divorce, neither spouse has to accuse the other of marital misconduct; if the marriage has broken down due to irreconcilable differences, the couple can get a divorce.

The No-Fault divorce or dissolution of marriage can be granted if the court finds that "irreconcilable differences" have caused an irrevocable breakdown of the marriage. This means that a married person who wants to end the marriage can do so, even if the other spouse wants to stay together.

Residency may be required in order to obtain dissolution of marriage. There may be a requirement that at least one of the spouses has been a resident of the state for at least six months before filing the divorce petition. You must also live in the county where you file the divorce petition for at least three months before filing.

It is governed by state, not national, law so you need to find a local attorney. Yes, you can get a quick divorce in Nevada, but you still have to go to their courts.

Government pages of a few states for your information:

http://www.courts.ca.gov/selfhelp-divorce.htm

http://www.wicourts.gov/ecourts/prose.htm

http://www.courts.wa.gov/forms/

http://courts.oregon.gov/OJD/OSCA/cpsd/courtimprovement/familylaw/Pages/FL_Divorce.aspx

http://www.clarkcountynv.gov/recorder/Pages/Divorce.aspx

https://supremecourt.nebraska.gov/self-help/7230/filing-divorce-nebraska-no-children-and-no-disputed-property

https://supremecourt.nebraska.gov/self-help/7230/filing-divorce-nebraska-no-children-and-no-disputed-property

When your marriage breaks up, the last thing you feel

like doing is crunching numbers. You're hurt, perhaps angry, and possibly overwhelmed with anxiety, fear, and despair. You're focused on the past and present, not the future.

But as many divorced couples have learned the hard way, this is precisely the time you need to get a grip and pay close attention to your assets and your financial future, lest both slip away in the flood of emotion. Since money is the No. 1 cause of divorce, it's safe to assume that splitting the financial sheets won't be easy. Here are 10 steps to help you cast off, steady your financial ship, and set sail for the solo voyage ahead:

1. Pull your credit report.

2. Open individual bank, credit card, and brokerage accounts.

3. Close all joint accounts.

4. Keep separate property separate.

5. Consider selling the house.

6. Change those beneficiaries.

7. Reclaim your name.

8. Check your retirement.

9. Guard your health coverage.

10. Dust yourself off and start living.

1. Pull your credit report.

Pull your credit report before the divorce so that anything in dispute can be resolved before the divorce is final. There are three major credit reporting agencies: Experian, TransUnion, and Equifax. Be sure to get a copy of your report from each of them. The reports are the quickest and easiest way to get an overview of the outstanding loan balances, mortgages, and credit card debt that you and your spouse will eventually divvy up.

2. Open individual bank, credit card, and brokerage accounts.

You also need to do this before the breakup is official. It will be easier to get a credit card and bank account in your own name while you are still married and share joint assets and debt on credit cards, mortgages and loans.

3. Close all joint accounts.

A divorce can take time. To avoid acquiring additional joint debt (or suddenly losing shared bank assets) during the legal process, close your joint credit card and bank accounts. You will, however, still be jointly responsible for paying off the balance of the closed accounts. Cancel the accounts in writing and be sure to request that they report each account as "closed by customer" to the credit bureaus.

Closing shared accounts is a critical step, and one that is too often overlooked. The more you remain connected to your ex-spouse financially, the more you are at risk. If possible, pay off joint credit card balances by check from your individual bank accounts or through balance transfers to your individual credit card accounts.

In a property-settlement agreement, couples often split their debt. One person takes the MasterCard and another, the American Express. It is an agreement between the two of you, not between you and the credit card company. You might be better off each borrowing in your own name and each paying off the credit cards so that you come out of the marriage without any joint debt.

4. Keep separate property separate.

Assets you brought to the marriage separately (real estate, vehicles, inheritance, gifts, money you acquired before marriage, etc.) are yours to take away from the marriage. If you put any separate assets into a joint account, they may be considered joint property.

Separate debt also travels with you. For example, if you brought a student loan into the marriage, you carry it out with you, even if your spouse was helping to pay it off.

5. Consider selling the house.

Traditionally, women try to keep the family home at all costs. Unfortunately, it's often an emotional decision that makes poor financial sense. For example, women have a hard time qualifying for a new mortgage usually because they have not worked as long or do not have a long working history as their male counterpart and the mortgage lenders will make it extremely difficult to qualify. This leads to making loans with interest double what you would pay otherwise creating high interest and with private lenders. Make sure you find out how, what and who you want as a company to apply for a mortgage.

6. Change those beneficiaries.

Despite what your divorce decrees, if you don't change the beneficiaries on your will, trusts, IRAs, pension plan, and life insurance, your ex could wind up with an unexpected windfall in the event of your untimely demise. As long as you're at it, this is a good time to review your various policies to make sure they fit with your new circumstances. And don't forget to delete your ex-spouse from these documents and policies and to change your marital status where applicable.

7. Reclaim your name.

For some women, divorce adds another task: reclaiming your name. If you are reverting to your maiden name, you may be required to produce the divorce decree or document signed by your ex-husband that acknowledges your new name in order to obtain a new driver's license, passport, or other identification. Use your new name to announce your new marital status to your circle of contacts: doctors, employer, human resources department, children's teachers, landlord, pharmacist, mail person, health insurer, and clergy.

Don't forget to register your name change (and adjust your withholding if needed) on your W-4 and other tax forms and with the Social Security Administration. A mix-up could cause you to lose valuable Social Security credits for your work, and you may have to show proof of both names when applying for benefits.

8. Check your retirement.

Speaking of Social Security, if divorce finds you within chipping distance of retirement, you will want to contact the Social Security Administration. If you are 62, were married for at least 10 years, have been divorced more than two years, and have not remarried, you may receive benefits based on your ex-spouse's Social Security record, even if he or she has not applied for benefits. If you are raising a child younger than 16 years old from the marriage, you may receive benefits on your ex-spouse's record even if you were married for less than 10 years. In most cases, you can expect the same amount you would have gotten if you had remained married (and possibly all of it if your ex-spouse dies). The benefits you draw do not affect amounts due to your ex's current spouse.

9. Guard your health coverage.

Sadly, divorce often forces one party to sacrifice health care coverage. Don't let this happen to you. One uncovered medical emergency can cripple your finances. Under the COBRA program, you are guaranteed 18 months of health coverage, albeit at rates that might induce cardiac irregularities. If you have no other avenue for affordable coverage, keep the COBRA plan in place until you find one.

10. Dust yourself off and start living.

Yes, you've survived a train wreck. If you accomplished most of these steps, you are more aware than you've ever been of your true financial picture and what you need to do about it.

If you receive a lump-sum payout, don't splurge for revenge or because you feel you deserve it. There is a wealth of financial planning help online. When you're ready, consider hiring a Certified Financial Planner to help you sort out your newly single money situation.

Financial experts recommend that you pull your credit report three months after the divorce and clean up any loose ends.

Family-Children-Friends

Certainly, a divorce is hardest on the couple and their children. But its effects can ripple out into the splitting of spouses' social spheres which often causes disruptions among friends and family members who aren't sure what they should say or do. Etiquette, like anything else, is complicated, but why is divorce etiquette so tricky? "It has to do with our emotional reaction to a close friend or family member's divorce," says Margot Swann, founder and director of Visions Anew, a nonprofit divorce resource for women; "We don't like the picture changing, which makes us feel awkward." Plus, she adds, it might bring up uncomfortable feelings about our own marriage. If it can happen to them...

Let's take a look at fourteen issues that may happen.

1. A good friend just told you that she's getting a divorce, and you don't know the right way to respond.

The best thing you can say is a simple: "I'm here for you." Since this is a death of a marriage and life style, your support for a divorcing friend is like being there for someone who is grieving after a death. Margot Swann says the easiest way to provide support is to take your cues from her: If she wants to just spend time with you without talking about her ex, do that. If she needs a few late-night sessions to vent and work through her grief, be there for her. If she just wants a little company, offer to take her along on your morning walks or to the gym; come by with coffee (or a bottle of wine!) if she can't get a sitter. Don't forget she may need practical help, too; Swann suggests offering to drive her kid’s places or asking your husband to help out with chores like mowing the lawn or getting the oil changed in her car.

2. Your sibling is getting a divorce, but you think they are making a mistake.

In truth, you don't know - and never will know - if someone’s divorce is truly a mistake because none of us really understand what goes on behind closed doors. Even if you are aware that one of them had an affair, for example, you still don't know what caused them to stray.

Keep in mind that just because the news comes as a shock to you, the same might not apply for them; they may have been thinking about it and discussing it with their spouse for years before the announcement. One thing is certain: berating them for making a mistake won't help, says Swann. However, “you might want to ask if they tried couple's counseling,” Says Darlene Lancer, JD, MFT, a former attorney who's now a licensed marriage and family therapist, “Steer clear of offering advice that's not asked for. Stick to support."

3. The couple you and your husband always go on double dates with is now divorcing, and you two don't know whose side you should be on.

Try not to choose sides or leave them out. When people divorce, they often find they lose friends and are suddenly not invited to events they would normally attend. What a shame, Says Swann. As a friend, it is not your job to take sides; your job is to be supportive. Be sensitive to both of a divorcing couple's feelings. Don't rehash the past. Assure them that if they want to talk, you will take everything they say in strict confidence.

4. Your brother is getting a divorce but you've grown close to your former sister-in-law and want to remain friends with her.

You can continue being friends, but the social etiquette can be rough. Obviously, she will no longer be hanging out with you at family functions. It's now best to meet as pals, just the two of you. While the divorce is new, it is probably best to not include her in larger social gatherings.

If your brother is upset that you are still friendly his ex, be respectful of his feelings. Swann suggests saying "I'm sorry you feel that way, but I still enjoy spending time with Jane. I hope you understand," If your brother is adamant about you breaking it off, you may have to decide if the friendship is worth risking your relationship with your brother, adds Lancer. Support is just that. Do not give advice. Stay out of their fight. You are there to listen. A big part of a divorced life can be isolation and loneliness. So, stay close, but don't take sides.

5. Protecting children from trauma.

Negotiation and settlement is achieved by 99% of all resolved. Children need parents to make cooperative decisions and relationship. With appropriate choices at the beginning the children will have less pain and trauma.

6. If it's your divorce, ask for help.

No one can read your mind. You do not have to tell everyone you know what is going on but don't keep it all to yourself. Limit to a few trusted family or friends. But still, let them help you.

The process of divorce can leave family members feeling angry, hurt, confused, and discouraged. Many family members wonder if life will ever feel normal again. They worry about their future. We know that children of divorce are more vulnerable to depression, behavior problems, and problems in their own relationships. Parents are more likely to experience financial stress, depression, and problems in future relationships, including an even higher rate of divorce for second marriages. Divorce can throw families into months, even years of painful turmoil. Get help and ask for help there is no shame in doing so.

7. Income after divorce.

What kind of income are you able to generate all by yourself?

When you made your divorce agreement, did you consider the fact that you've never worked or that you've been out of the workforce for a significant amount of time? You may need training or retraining, even if you've been absent for a mere three years. Make sure you have indicated this as part of your settlement so that you have time and money to train for a job.

If you have been married for 10 years, you will qualify for your spouse's social security. However, if your spouse is not of age nor enrolled in their social security benefits program, you will not be able to collect.

Make sure you have considered your living expenses and how much you will need. Do you qualify for alimony? Hopefully this is something you can negotiate especially for the period of time for retraining and job search.

8. Therapists.

There is always help available. You can check your local directory or Google to find a therapist in your area that can help you make good decisions and avoid as many mistakes as possible. Take care of yourself as this is very stressful process. If you meditate, do it often. If you don't mediate, now is a good time to learn. Research the best, most comfortable methods and make this part of your daily routine. BREATHE!

9. Attorney or DIY?

Can you manage a divorce yourself? You can usually do it yourself if you have been married fewer than five years and have no assets and no children. If this is not your situation, you need to find a good divorce attorney and a good Certified Divorce Financial Analyst (CDFA). If you have decided to see how far you can go on your own, check the previously mentioned links for help.

10. Documentation.

Before announcing you want a divorce, make sure you have gathered all your papers and documents. You'll need: a passport, bank statements, investment statements, tax returns for the past three years, credit card statements, mortgage and other debt statements, wills and trust, insurance policies, property title and any other statement of ownership.

11. Division of Property.

This is calculated based on ownership of all properties and debts. Make sure you no longer have the mortgage in both your names. If you don't, you'll still be married through mortgage. Splitting the house will be based on fair market value, the potential future value, and length of time the assets will last to provide a lifetime of income. Find a CDFA® to help you make decisions on your debt and assets.

12. Beneficiary Estate Insurance Title.

Make sure you have changed your will, trust, and all your beneficiaries and have also changed titles to your assets. You do not want to have the wrong person inherit your estate, especially if you don't like them anymore and you have family that should inherit. *I have repeated this because this seems the area were everyone seems to procrastinate and do not get it done.*

13. Moving out of the state or the country.

Moving may be what you need, however, if you have children and joint custody, this may be tricky. You will need to make sure the other parent has been notified of your move and agrees. If not, you will end up in court to resolve the issue. Moving out of the country entirely is drastic, and you'll need family and friends who can support you if not financially, then emotionally. You need to research the country as well as your ability to generate income and a place to live. Will you be able to secure medical coverage? What about the weather? This kind of move is probably best if you are returning to your home country. It is very costly to move and could be a great opportunity for a great adventure just plan and map it out.

14. Divorce-Taxes-Tax Planning.

Tax planning and doing your taxes is an important yet complicated issue. How to file? Filing jointly, filing separately or head of household truly depends on the circumstances of your situation. You also need to make sure your divorce degree states how you will deal with naming the custodial parent, child support terms, and who and when the child exemption is used. Finding a tax professional, EA (Enrolled Agent), or CPA to help you make decisions and avoid costly mistakes is a must and is worth the cost of a consultation. Even in a divorce situation, you don't want to pay the IRS more than you need to.

References:

IRS Pub. 504: Divorced or Separated Individuals.

IRC §71: Alimony and separate maintenance payments.

IRC §215: Alimony, etc., payments.

IRC §414(p): Qualified domestic relations order defined.

IRC §1041: Transfers of property between spouses or incident to divorce

For property settlements and transfers, no gain or loss is recognized on:

Transfers between spouses.

Transfers between former spouses if incident to divorce.

This rule applies even if the transfer is exchange for cash, release of marital rights, assumption of liabilities, or other consideration.

Transfers are incident to divorce if they are:

Made within one year after the date the marriage ends,

or

Related to the ending of the marriage - made under an original or modified divorce or separation instrument within six years after the date the marriage ends.

Transfers that do not meet these conditions are presumed not to be related to the ending of the marriage, but see Regulation Section 1.1041-1T (Q&A 7) and PLR 200442003 for information on rebutting the presumption. Transfer to a third party. Non-recognition may also apply to a transfer on behalf of a spouse or former spouse. See IRS Pub. 504 Divorced or Separated Individuals.

Distributions from qualified retirement plans and tax-sheltered annuities are taxable to the plan participant and subject to early withdrawal penalties unless made to an alternate payee under a Qualified Domestic Relations Order (QDRO). A QDRO is a judgment, decree, or court order issued under a state's domestic relations law that must state the following provisions:

Someone other than the participant has a right to receive benefits from a qualified retirement plan or a tax-sheltered annuity

Payment of child support, alimony, or martial property rights are to be paid to a spouse, former spouse, child, or other dependent of the participant

The actual amount or a part of the participant's benefits are to be paid to the participant's spouse, former spouse, child, or other dependent.

Distributions under a QDRO are taxable to the recipient spouse but are not subject to early withdrawal penalties. Qualifying distributions can be rolled over. The recipient spouse may elect lump sum treatment if available. The recipient receives a share of the participant's investment in the contract, if any, to figure the taxable amount. Benefits paid to a participant's child or other dependent under a QDRO are taxable to the participant but are not subject to early withdrawal penalties.

Example: According to an addendum to their divorce decree, the taxpayer deposited pension distributions into a joint account with his ex-wife for her exclusive benefit. He did not report the pension distributions on his income tax return. The Tax Court held the addendum failed to be a QDRO because direct payment was not made to the ex-wife as an alternate payee.

Distributions were taxable income for the taxpayer even though his ex-wife actually received the money. (Hackenberg, T.C. Summary 2010-135). Transfer to a spouse under a divorce or separation instrument is not a taxable transfer. Transfers can be made by direct transfer from trustee to trustee or by changing ownership of the IRA account. A QDRO is not required. The IRA is treated as the recipient's as of the date of transfer. IRA distributions are subject to early withdrawal penalties even when the distribution is court ordered. The penalty exception for payments to an alternate payee under a QDRO does not apply to IRAs.

Sale of residence.

For purposes of the IRC section 121 exclusion of gain, an owner is treated as using property as his or her principal residence during any period that use is granted to a spouse or former spouse under a divorce or separation instrument. To process a QDRO the company benefit plan will charge a fee to process in some case the cost is $750 to $2000. Before starting the process, find out what the company's benefit plan will charge. This will avoid an unpleasant surprise. You can also include this cost in your negotiation. In any case, mention the benefit plan and see what you qualify for. All you can do is ask. As Nora Roberts said, "If you do not ask, the answer is always a no."

15. Cost of Divorce

Generally, attorneys' fees and other expenses paid in connection with divorce are not deductible. Exceptions:

> Fees paid to determine tax or for tax advice on federal, state, or local taxes of any type are deductible.
>
> Fees paid to get or collect alimony are deductible. Fees paid for a spouse or former spouse are not deductible but may qualify as alimony.

Alimony is a payment to or for a spouse or former spouse under a divorce or separation instrument. Note: It does not include voluntary payments not made under the instrument. Alimony is deductible by the payer and must be included in the recipient's income. To be considered alimony, a payment must meet certain requirements. For payments made under instruments executed before 1985, see IRS Pub. 504 Divorced or Separated Individuals.

Alimony

Payments are alimony if ALL the following are true:

Payments are required by a divorce or separation instrument.

Payer and recipient spouse do not file a joint return.

Payment is in cash (including checks and money orders).

Payments not considered to be in cash include noncash property settlements, spouse's part of community income, and upkeep for the payer's property, and use of the payer's property.

Payment is not designated in the instrument as "not alimony."

Divorced and legally separated spouses are not members of the same household when payment is made.

Payments are not required after death of the recipient spouse.

Payment is not treated as child support.

A house formerly shared by the spouses is considered one household. Spouses are not treated as members of the same household if one spouse is preparing to leave and does in fact leave no later than one month after payment. Until divorce or legal separation is final, spouses can be members of the same household. If payments can continue after death, the part of the payment that would continue is not alimony whether made before or after death. The divorce or separation instrument does not need to expressly state that payment ceases if liability for payments ends by operation of state law.

Designating payments as "not alimony." Spouses can agree not to treat qualifying payments as alimony. Alimony Recapture - reduction in first three years: In some cases, if the alimony paid in the second and/or third year decreases from that paid in a prior year, alimony must be recaptured. Many more rules apply it would be important to review with your tax professional.

10.

Strategies for Investing Opportunities and Possibilities

The question isn't "Should I invest?" The question is "How much should I invest and where?" My job is to help you understand the different aspects of investing and to realize achieving wealth, diversification, and long-term security requires investing.

Small steps are the best way to start as we are more apt to stick with it; big steps can hurt and seem unachievable which leads to giving up the plan.

As previously stated in chapter 2 start with $300,000 as a goal. When you reach that amount, celebrate! And now save for the next $300,000 and next, etc. While a million is overwhelming, $300,000 is achievable. We can count to 300,000 more easily and quickly.

Now how should you start? If you decide to invest in the stock market, make sure you have the time and tolerance. This kind of investing is best if you don't need your money for ten or more years. Don't try to "time" the market. Timing the market is very risky and not worth your time or money as losses can be enormous. Invest for the long term and make it your serious money (your important savings for the future not to gamble with) this is advice only for people who are serious and are committed to three things: time, money, and mindset.

When you are saving for a vacation, car, or the down payment to purchase a home, this is a short-term investment. For short term savings use savings accounts and CD's at a bank or credit union. When you reach $50,000 to invest, now you can look for longer term investment vehicles. You can work with a brokerage or other options. It is a matter of finding the right people to work with.

Savings Accounts

Savings can be an old fashion piggy bank, envelope, or any place you can keep money safe until you can open an account. You can open an account at a brick and mortar bank or an online bank to keep your money safe as well as earn a tiny bit of interest. Interest is what the bank is willing to pay for an account without restrictions.

A savings account is helpful because you can access your money at any time after your initial deposit. Shop around and find a bank willing to pay you for keeping your money in their bank. You usually need $100 - $300 to open an account and not be charged. This savings is insured for $250,000 per account registration through FDIC (Federal Deposit Insurance Corporation). See www.fdic.gov/deposit/ for more details.

CD's Certificate of Deposit

You can purchase CD's (Certificate of Deposits) in banks, credit unions, NCUA (www.ncua.gov/), through your Investment advisor, CFP® and thrift institutions. They are very much like a savings account except they have different terms. For example, you must keep your money in a 3-, 6-, 9-, 12-month, or 1-5-year CD. Should you want your money sooner, there is a penalty for withdrawing before the maturity date. The penalty for early withdrawal can be as high as six months of interest. By agreeing to keep your money in the bank until maturity, you will receive the full interest the bank has promised on the CD's.

Keeping your money in a CD means there is no risk of

losing original deposit, changing the agreed upon interest, or being subjected to fluctuation. The risk is purchasing power. If you do not beat inflation or taxation, you have lost purchasing power and potentially will run out of money sooner than other investments.

Equity Markets

A stock is an investment that represents ownership in a corporation. This means you own a piece of the corporation and as a stockholder, you have the right to receive profits from the corporation if the board declares that dividends will be paid. You also have a claim on the corporation's assets.

There are two types of stocks, Common and Preferred. Common Stock owners receive dividends and have the right to vote. Owners of Preferred Stocks have no rights to vote however, they are the first in line to be paid higher dividends and have a higher claim on assets in the event of bankruptcy.

If a company has 1,000 shares of stock outstanding and if you buy 100 shares, you now have a 10% ownership in the company and a 10% claim on the company's assets. Note that it is more effective to own as many shares as possible because, when stocks pay dividends, they do not pay off the value of the stock but on how many shares you own.

Stocks are subject to Commodity Price Risk, Headline Risk, Rating Risk, Obsolescence Risk, Detection Risk, Legislature Risk, Inflationary Risk, Interest Risk, Model Risk, and the bottom line risk. (http://www.investopedia.com/contributors/82/)

Stocks are the foundation of nearly every portfolio. Historically, they have outperformed most other investments over the long run; however, there is no guarantee.

You, the investor, need to decide what kind of risk you want to take and decide which stock options you want to own. Speaking to a certified financial planner will help you make this decision.

Bonds

A bond is a fixed investment. Instead of owning a partial part of the company, the investor lends the money to a company for a fixed period of time. You can invest in corporations, government, municipalities, and other entities by lending your money with the promise of full investment returns and dividends upon maturity.

Bonds are commonly referred to as fixed-income securities and are one of the three main common asset classes, along with stocks (equities) and cash equivalents. Many corporate and government bonds are publicly traded on exchanges, while others are traded only over the counter.

Bonds are traded just like stocks, so changes in the economy and the markets can cause bond prices to rise or fall. Bonds are subject to the usual risks of inflation, credit, and interest rate changes. When interest rates rise, bond prices fall.

If interest rates drop to 4%, the bond will continue paying out at 5%, making it a more attractive option. Investors will purchase these bonds, bidding the price up to a premium until the effective rate on the bond equals 4%.

On the other hand, if interest rates rise to 6%, the 5% coupon is no longer attractive and the bond price will decrease, selling at a discount until it's effective rate is 6%. Because of this mechanism, bond prices move inversely with interest rates.

Like a teeter-totter, one side goes up as the other side goes down. When companies or other entities need to raise money to finance new projects, maintain ongoing operations, or refinance existing debts, they may issue bonds directly to investors instead of obtaining loans from a bank. The indebted entity (i.e. the issuer) issues a bond that contractually states the interest rate (i.e. the coupon) that will be paid and the time at which the loaned funds must be returned (i.e. the maturity date).

The issuance price of a bond is typically set at par,

usually $100 or $1,000 face value per individual bond. The actual market price of a bond depends on a number of factors including the credit quality of the issuer, the length of time until expiration, and the coupon rate compared to the general interest rate environment at the time.

Because fixed-rate coupon bonds will pay the same percentage of its face value over time, the market price of the bond will fluctuate as that coupon becomes desirable or undesirable given prevailing interest rates at a given moment in time.

For example, if a bond is issued when prevailing interest rates are 5% at $1,000 par value with a 5% annual coupon, it will generate $50 of cash flows per year. To the bondholder (the owner of the bond). The bond holder earns the same return as if the money was parked in a savings account.

Most bonds share some common basic characteristics including:

Face value - The money amount the bond will be worth at its maturity, and is also the reference amount the bond issuer uses when calculating interest payments.

Coupon rate - The rate of interest the bond issuer will pay on the face value of the bond, expressed as a percentage.

Coupon dates - The dates on which the bond issuer will make interest payments. Typical intervals are annual or semi-annual coupon payments.

Maturity date - The date the bond will mature. On this date, the bond issuer will pay the bond holder the face value of the bond.

Issue price - The price at which the bond issuer originally sells the bonds.

There are two features of a bond: credit quality and duration. If the issuer has a poor credit rating, the risk of default is greater and these bonds will tend to trade a discounted rate. Credit ratings are calculated and issued by credit rating agencies. Bond maturities can range from less than a day to more than 30 years. The longer the bond maturity (i.e. the duration), the greater the chances of adverse effects. Longer-dated bonds also tend to have lower liquidity is the ability to get to cash out and have the use of the funds or the cash it provides for another purchase with stability.

Because of these attributes, bonds with a longer time to maturity typically command a higher interest rate. When considering the riskiness of bond portfolios, investors typically consider the duration and curvature of duration (essentially, how the bond value changes as interest rates change).

There are three main categories of bonds:

Corporate bonds issued by companies.

Municipal bonds issued by states and municipalities. Municipal bonds can offer tax-free coupon income for residents of those municipalities.

U.S. Treasury bonds (more than 10 years to maturity), notes (1-10 years to maturity) and bills (less than one year to maturity). These are collectively referred to as "Treasuries."

Varieties of Bonds

Zero-coupon bonds do not pay out regular coupon payments and instead are issued at a discount. Their market price eventually converges to face value upon maturity. The discount a zero-coupon bond sells for will be equivalent to the yield of a similar coupon bond.

Convertible bonds are debt instruments with an embedded call option that allows bondholders to convert their debt into stock at some point if the share price rises to a sufficiently high level.

Callable bonds: Some corporate bonds are callable, meaning that the company can call back the bonds from debt holders if interest rates drop sufficiently. These bonds typically trade at a premium to non-callable debt due to the risk of being called away and also due to their relative scarcity in today's bond market. Other bonds are puttable, meaning that creditors can put the bond back to the issuer if interest rates rise sufficiently.

Bullet bonds make up the majority of today's corporate market. They have no embedded options and the entire face value is paid out at once upon maturity. (From Investopedia)

ETF's

In the simplest terms, Exchange Traded Funds (ETFs) are funds that track indexes like the NASDAQ-100 Index, S&P 500, Dow Jones, etc. When you buy shares of an ETF, you are buying shares of a portfolio that tracks the yield and return of its native index. The main difference between ETFs and other types of index funds is that ETFs don't try to outperform their corresponding index, but simply replicate its performance. They don't try to beat the market; they try to be the market. ETFs have been around since the early 1980s, but they've come into their own within the past 10 years.

ETFs combine the range of a diversified portfolio with the simplicity of trading a single stock. Investors can purchase and trade an ETF just like stocks. Since ETF tracks an index without trying to outperform it, it incurs fewer administrative costs than actively managed portfolios. Actively managed portfolios experience the trading of securities, which can create potentially high capital gains distributions. Fewer trades in and out of the trust mean fewer taxable distributions, and a more efficient overall return on investments.

Efficiency is one reason ETFs have become a favored vehicle for multiple investment strategies - because lower administrative costs and lower capital gains taxes put a greater share of your investment dollar to work in the market.

ETF shares trade exactly like stocks. Passive management is also an advantage in terms of tax efficiency. Mutual funds are priced only after market closings; ETFs are priced and traded continuously throughout the trading day. They can be bought on margin, sold short, or held for the long-term, exactly like common stock.

Yet because their value is based on an underlying index, ETFs enjoy the additional benefits of broader diversification than shares in single companies, as well as what many investors perceive as the greater flexibility that goes with investing in entire markets, sectors, regions, or asset types.

Because they represent baskets of stocks, ETFs based on major indexes typically trade at much higher volumes than individual stocks. High trading volumes mean high liquidity, enabling investors to get into and out of investment positions with minimum risk and expense.

A stock market index is a list of related stocks, together

with statistics representing their aggregate value. A stock market index is used chiefly as a benchmark for indicating the value of its component stocks, as well as investment vehicles, such as mutual funds, that hold positions in those stocks.

Indexes can be based on various categories of stocks. There are the widely-known market indexes, such as the Dow Jones Industrial Average, the NASDAQ Composite, or the S&P 500. There are indexes based on market sectors, such as tech, healthcare, financial, foreign markets, market cap (micro-, small-, mid-, large-, and mega-cap), asset type (small growth, large growth, etc.), and even commodities.

Mutual Funds

Mutual funds are investments that allow you to pool your money together with other investors to purchase a collection of stocks, bonds, or other securities. The price of the mutual fund, also known as its net asset value (NAV), is determined by the total value of the securities in the portfolio divided by the number of the fund's outstanding shares at the end of the business trading day. This price fluctuates based on the value of the securities held by the portfolio at the end of each business day.

Note: mutual fund investors do not actually own the securities in which the fund invests; they only own shares in the fund itself.

The primary goal of the investment manager is to outperform its benchmark (a method of measuring the performance of a mutual fund by using indexes like the Standard & Poor's 500 or the Russell 2000) which followed indexes like the Standard & Poor's 500 or the Russell 2000.

If you have a small amount to invest, a mutual fund is a good way to start as they are cost effective. Most mutual funds allow a $2,000 initial investment and contributions of $50 a month (you can contribute more, of course). This is also a simple way to diversify your portfolio and get started in the stock market.

Life Insurance & Annuities as Investments

Life insurance is usually thought of as a death benefit, but in the 80s and 90s, the trend was to buy Term Insurance and invest the difference. Term insurance is usually cheaper to purchase as the gamble from the insurance side you will not die by the time the term is finish and they do not payout. While an insurance that has cash value cost more because you have the use of the cash value for loan.

The difference of term or whole life is what they recommended you could invest. For example, if term cost $20 and whole life $100 the difference of $80 you would invest and be ahead of the game. After a decade or two, people came to realize this does not work. The average investor is not disciplined enough to invest the difference. Some investors even ran out of life insurance since terms can end in 10, 20, or 30 years.

Many people don't realize they can outlive their insurance even though their loved one still needs it. Plus, you may find you are too old or unhealthy to qualify for a new insurance policy. Remember you may be able to pay for insurance but you cannot buy it unless you are healthy and young enough. Like investing, insurance is most affordable early. The perfect time to buy a life insurance policy is when you don't need it.

Adjustable or Universal Life Insurance

When you buy adjustable or universal life insurance, you have an opportunity to extend your policy up to age 100. You can also use your policy to accumulate a great deal of cash to pay for college (or other goals) without paying taxes. Life insurance is one of the last vehicles that is not usually taxable. This kind of investment is great opportunity to increase your wealth and help your loved ones.

Variable Life Insurance is an insurance policy with a death benefit that offers permanent life insurance, flexible premiums, and the ability to build cash value. You have the opportunity to accumulate cash value by choosing from a variety of investment options across risk categories. Variable life policies have the potential for greater cash value growth than other types of life insurance. However, they can also lose cash value (that would be the variable part). If you're comfortable with market fluctuations, this type of policy may be an option to consider.

Annuities: Fixed and Variable

Here is a true story. In the '90s, clients James and Flora were retiring from their positions at a national bank. They had a lump sum of $65,000. At 60, James was very concerned this amount would not be enough to protect his Flora and their son who had special needs.

We discussed different possibilities and opportunities to protect the family and agreed that a variable annuity with guaranteed step-up every anniversary year would be the best for what he wanted to achieve. This annuity would allow about a 10% withdraw without penalties. By 2003 their investment had grown to $120,000. But then, the market plunged. The annuity dropped to about $89,000.

Flora was especially concerned and wanted to take it all out. I asked her and James what was the purpose for this annuity, and they replied that it was the death benefit. I then reminded them that if they took the money out they would no longer have the death benefit of $120,000. Flora would lose that gain, ending up with only $89,000 to deposit in a bank CD. James and she agreed that it would not be a good idea to do this as they would lose the death benefit.

Shortly after this conversation, James was diagnosed with cancer and died. Flora received the death benefit of $120,000, minus the withdraw of $10,000 that they took out for a new car. This annuity achieved several purposes: nontaxable growth, protection from a down market, and most importantly the death benefits the client needed and wanted. Had Flora responded to the market down turn and pulled the annuity, she would have lost $31,000.

Annuities are part of the insurance family. In fact, they are a contract between the insurance company and the annuitant. They provide certain benefits depending of choices and expenses you are willing to pay for and the different products that insurance company offers. They mainly provide for a death benefit and guaranteed income.

They are tax deferred until you withdraw the money, and they are subject to IRS penalties for withdrawing the money prior to reaching the age of 59 1/2. This is one of the few products that can help put money into a deferred plan with no taxes to pay until withdrawal.

Annuities can be used for IRA's, IRA rollovers, 403 (b) and 401 (k) retirement plans, as well as to provide protection against taxes, provide death benefits, and guaranteed income. If after a sale, inheritance, or gambling winnings you have $100,000, invest that money into an annuity guaranteeing income paid out from these funds. As long as the money is inside the annuity, no taxes are paid. When you finally do withdraw the money, that amount is taxable (you will receive a 1099R form).

Annuities are not for everyone, and you should make sure that this investment product is the best choice.

Real Estate Investment - Your Home vs Rental Property

Your home is not considered an investment to be used for increasing wealth. In fact, as a Financial Planner, I never consider that asset as something to calculate in when trying to create income and increase wealth. Your home is the American Dream, and you must live, somewhere right? Your home is your home, and while you may be able to use the value of it, it does not build wealth in itself. It builds security, a sense of ownership, a feeling of wellbeing and confidence, and a place you belong. Should you sell this home, where are you going to live? Are you going to rent? Are you going to want to use it for a reverse mortgage because you have no other asset to sustain you?

A reverse mortgage should be considered a last resort - you must be living in your home, and you cannot leave or you owe back the money. You can also run out of money because you have outlived the source. You will then need to make payments or sell to repay. Your family will need to pay it back should they want to keep your home. So, unless they have the money or can qualify for a loan, the home is gone.

Using your home to borrow to pay off things like credit cards is a disaster waiting to happen. Think about it - you are using long term debt to pay for short term items, and you will probably never pay it off. This puts a burden on both the asset and you. Short term debt and loans can start at a repayment as short as a week, 90 days to 10 years and long-term debt is 10 years and up from there.

Residential rental properties play a significant role in the economy of the United States. They provide a valuable source of living accommodations for members of society who either cannot afford their own home or who choose not to do so. According to the U.S. Census, in 2014 some 65% of families, over 200 million people, own their own homes, leaving 113 million in residential real estate housing of different types.

Because of supply and demand this may be a good investment to research and check out to see if you have the temperament and the capital to purchase residential rental properties. You should ask yourself what is my purpose, what do I want to happen, and is this kind of investment right for me.

Is this kind of property for rental income or do I want this property to appreciate and grow in value? Do I have the time and the expertise to fix and improve this property on my own or will I need to hire people to do the job? This kind of property, in the IRS code, is passive income and there are a lot of issues involved. You need a professional EA to help you with the declaration of income and expenses.

There are two things you need to consider before you make this investment, consider whether you are going to materially participate or actively participate. What does this mean? What IRS implications?

Generally speaking, a taxpayer is considered to have materially participated in an activity for the tax year if he or she was involved in its operations on a regular, continuous, and substantial basis during the year. (Straight from the IRS - Further details can be found in IRS Publication 925, Passive Activity and At-Risk Rules, or in the instructions for Schedule C and E.)

The IRS code also states that "Regarding a participating spouse, taxpayers who are married can also count any participation in the activity by their spouse when determining whether they materially participated in an activity during the year. This holds true even if the spouse owns no interest in the activity or files a separate return for the year."

Exception for Rental Real Estate with Active Participation

If a taxpayer or spouse actively participated in a passive

rental real estate activity, the taxpayer can deduct up to $25,000 of loss from the activity from his or her non-passive income. This special allowance is an exception to the general rule disallowing losses in excess of income from passive activities. Similarly, the taxpayer can offset credits from the activity against the tax on up to $25,000 of non-passive income after taking into account any losses allowed under this exception."

Example: Mary Beth is single with a $60,000 a year job. She also gets $1,000 a year of passive income from a limited Partnership. She has a rental that over the year has lost $4,000. Out of that passive income and loss, the $1,000 income offsets a $1,000 from the passive loss. That remaining 3,000 loss carries over to the next year to be used against other passive income. This works for Mary Beth because she is single. Be careful about your own filing status and check all the options before filing.

Active Participation

This is a rental term. The IRS considers you an active participant in a rental property if you own at least 10% of the property, make decisions about the property (like rent terms and approving tenants) and/or arrange for services (like maintenance and repairs).

Maximum Special Allowance

The maximum special allowance is:

$25,000 for single individuals and married individuals filing a joint return for the tax year

$12,500 for married individuals who file separate returns for the tax year and lived apart from their spouses at all times during the tax year.

$25,000 for a qualifying estate reduced by the special allowance for which the surviving spouse qualified.

When you have a Modified Adjusted Gross Income (MAGI) of $100,000 or less ($50,000 or less if you and your spouse file separately), you can deduct the Maximum Special Allowance. If you are lucky and have a MAGUS of more than $100,000 (more than $50,000 if filing separately), your special allowance is limited to 50% of the difference between $150,000 ($75,000 if married filing separately).

If your income is over $100,000, the MAGI may not be a good idea as you are limited by what you can deduct. Most investors count on asset depreciation as a deduction off ordinary income. Investors can deduct up to $25,000. If the amount is not deducted during that year, the expense is carried over for the next year. This can continue on until you sell the property and use the unallowable losses to offset gains.

This kind of investment is complicated and needs a professional EA or CPA to make sure you are in compliance with the IRS Code.

Antiques & Collectibles

This kind of an asset is usually easier to buy than to sell. To make a wise investment, you need to know a lot about these collectibles in order to understand their value. One of the disadvantages is the items are taxed at the highest rate 28% at the capital gain tax rate instead of at other asset tax rates, which can be as low as 15% or 20%. Additionally, to make a gain on your antique, you need a willing buyer who agrees with you on value and price. The market may be very narrow, and this item may not be able to be sold quickly.

We collect things because we have an emotional attachment to the item and what it represents to us. Our things all have a story. For instance, I collect small versions of the Statue of Liberty. When I was five, my family, Dad, Mom, and my sister Margie and I sailed from France to New York on the *Constitution* (the same ship featured on "An Affair to Remember" with Debora Kerr and Cary Grant, 1956). My dad had not seen his parents for 9 years.

I remember sailing through the port of New York, my dad holding my hand, and there she was - the Statue of Liberty, so tall and beautiful. I do not remember what my father said, but to this day I can remember his warm hand in mine, the reverent murmur of his words, and the pure expression of his emotions as he arrived home.

This memory brings me to tears, and that's why I love

her, the Statue of Liberty. So, I collect everything about her. My clients bring me tokens of the Statue, and they honor me with their gifts. Fair Market Value is one thing but memories are quite another. She is my treasure.

Do you watch *Antiques Road Show*? This show lets you know how much your antique or collectible maybe worth, and it reminds you to pay attention to the items that have been in your family forever. Not everything you have has significant monetary value, and it shouldn't. Some of our collectibles represent our link with the past. They are a visual reminder of who we are and where we come from, just like the Statue of Liberty.

Alternative Investments

To qualify for most alternative investments, you need to make no less than $75,000 per year and have assets $250,000 or more, not including your residence. You cannot invest more than 10% of your portfolio. This asset class is not for everyone and should be properly checked for investment purposes.

REIT Real Estate Trust Public - from Hines Securities

REITs, an investment vehicle for real estate that is comparable to a mutual fund. It allows both small and large investors to acquire ownership in real estate ventures and in some cases, to operate commercial properties such as apartment complexes, hospitals, office buildings, timber land, warehouses, hotels, and shopping malls.

All REITs must have at least 100 shareholders, no five of whom can hold more than 50% of shares between them. At least 75% of a REIT's assets must be invested in real estate, cash or U.S. Treasury's; 75% of gross income must be derived from real estate.

REITs are required by law to maintain dividend payout ratios of at least 90%, making them a favorite for income-seeking investors. REITs can deduct these dividends and avoid most or all tax liabilities, though investors still pay income tax on the payouts they receive. Many REITs have dividend reinvestment plans (DRIPs), allowing returns to compound over time.

REIT History

REITs have existed for more than 50 years in the U.S. Congress granted legal authority to form REITs in 1960 as an amendment to the Cigar Excise Tax Extension of 1960. That year The National Association of Real Estate Investment Funds, a professional group for the promotion of REITs is founded. The following year it changed its name to the National Association of Real Estate Investment Trust (NAREIT).

In 1965 the first REIT, Continental Mortgage Investors,

is listed on the New York Stock Exchange (NYSE). By the late 1960s, major investors, including George Soros, became interested in research on the value of REITs. Mortgage based REITs account for much of the growth of REITs in the early 1970s, and they fuel a housing boom. The boom busts after the oil shocks of 1973 and the recession that follows.

In 1969 the first European REIT legislation (the Fiscal Investment Institution Regime [*fiscale beleggingsinstelling*: FBI]) is passed in The Netherlands.

International REITs

Since their development in Europe, REITs have become available in many countries outside the United States on every continent on Earth.

The first listed property trusts launch in Australia in 1971. Canadian REITs debut in 1993, but they don't become popular investment vehicles until the beginning of the 21st century. REITs began to spread across Asia with the launch of Japanese REITs in 2001. REITs in Europe were buoyed by legislation in France (2003), Germany (2007) and the U.K. (2007). In total, about 40 countries now have REIT legislation.

The 3 Main Kinds of REITs in the U.S.

1. Equity REITs invest in and own properties, that is,

they are responsible for the equity or value of their real estate assets. Their revenues come principally from leasing space - such as in an office building - to tenants. They then distribute the rents they've received as dividends to shareholders. Equity REITs may sell property holdings, in which case this capital appreciation is reflected in dividends. Timber REITs will include capital appreciation from timber sales in their dividends. Equity REITs account for the vast majority of REITs.

2. Mortgage REITs invest in and own property mortgages. These REITs loan money for mortgages to real estate owners, or purchase existing mortgages or mortgage-backed securities. Their earnings are generated primarily by the net interest margin, the spread between the interest they earn on mortgage loans and the cost of funding these loans. This model makes them potentially sensitive to interest rate increases. In general, mortgage REITs are less highly leveraged than other commercial mortgage lenders, using a relatively higher ration of equity to debt to fund themselves.

3. Hybrid REITs invest in both properties and mortgages. Individuals can invest in REITs either by purchasing their shares directly on an open exchange or by investing in a mutual fund that specializes in public real estate. Some REITs are SEC-registered and public, but not listed on an exchange; others are private.

Some REITs will invest specifically in one area of real estate - shopping malls, for example - or in one specific region, state or country. Others are more diversified. There are several REIT ETFs available, most of which have fairly low expense rations. The ETF format can help investors avoid over-dependence on one company, geographical area or industry.

REITs provide a liquid and non-capital-intensive way to invest in real estate. Many have dividend yields in excess of 10%. REITs are also largely uncorrelated with stocks and bonds, meaning they provide a measure of diversification.

REIT Real Estate Trust Private

Private REITs, sometimes referred to as private-placement REITs, are neither traded on a national stock exchange nor registered with the SEC. As a result, private REITs are not subject to the same disclosure requirements as stock exchange-listed or public non-listed REITs.

Private REITs issue shares that are neither traded on national exchanges nor registered with the SEC, but rather issued pursuant to one or more of several exemptions to the securities laws set forth in regulations promulgated and enforced by the SEC. These exemptions include rules set forth under Regulation D, permitting an issuer to sell securities to "accredited investors," and Rule 144A, which exempts securities issued to qualified institutional buyers (QIBs).

BDC Business Development Corporations

Note: I pulled from CNL Securties.com for the exact wording on Business Development Corporations. Look up CNLsecurities.com for more details on any of these categories.

A BDC is a company that invests primarily in the debt or equity of private American companies and has elected to be regulated by certain provisions under the Investment Company Act of 1940. A BDC combines the capital of many investors to own debt of or finance a portfolio of operating businesses.

The BDC structure was created in1980 by Congress to encourage capital investment into privately owned American businesses. At that time, much like today, the supply of capital for private companies was limited.

A BDC can elect to be taxed as a regulated investment company (RIC). To qualify as a RIC, it must distribute at least 90% of its taxable income to stockholders annually.

Investing in private companies has traditionally only been available to large institutions. The BDC structure now provides the investing public the ability to invest in a portfolio of private debt and private equity.

Investors participate in BDCs for a number of reasons,

including their use as a potential source of diversification within a portfolio, as private equity and private debt funds have historically exhibited imperfect correlation with traditional asset classes. Additionally, BDCs provide the potential for both current and long-term returns.

Investing in non-traded BDCs fits within the asset allocation fundamentals of most financial planning strategies, which recommend both traditional liquid and alternative less liquid investments in a portfolio.

Non-Traded BDCs

BDCs and REITs both invest in a portfolio of private alternative assets. Each publicly files detailed quarterly public financial reports.

They differ in that a REIT makes investments primarily by buying real estate and earns income from rent payments, while a BDC makes investments primarily by making loans to and purchasing equity from private companies. The BDC then collects interest payments or earnings from the private companies.

The real estate that REITs make investments in can include all sectors and stages of development. Those investments range from stabilized income producing properties to development or repositioning opportunities. Similarly, the private companies that BDCs make investments in can operate across any industry and all stages of development. They range from early-stage startups to corporations with billions of dollars in revenues and global name recognition.

Both vehicles are required to comply with Sarbanes-Oxley and have tax reporting on Form 1099. Each intends to distribute at least 90% of income.

BDC Compared to a real Estate Investment Trust (REIT)

A traded BDC is a public company whose shares are traded on major stock exchanges such as New York Stock Exchange or NASDAQ.

Non-traded BDCs are also public companies but their shares are not traded on major exchanges. Shareholder liquidity is not guaranteed and is provided on a limited interim basis.

Both traded and non-traded BDCs are required to calculate the fair market value of their portfolios on a quarterly basis based on a valuation process approved by their board of directors and subject to auditor or third-party review.

A traded BDC is generally subject to the daily volatility of the stock market, which can cause its share price to trade at a premium or discount to its book value.

A non-traded BDC is generally not subject to the immediate market volatility that being listed on a stock exchange causes. This structure enables a BDC to operate with a long-term view, instead of managing to quarterly market expectations, and to pursue its investment objectives without subjecting its shareholders to swings in market sentiment and the daily share price volatility associated with the public markets.

Traded BDC vs a Non-Traded BDC

BDCs are an efficient way for people to invest in a portfolio of private operating companies which would be otherwise unavailable.

This is another diversification tool as is evidenced by historically lower correlation between the alternative asset classes they invest in compared to traditional asset classes.

Investments in non-traded REITs or BDCs are subject to significant risks. These risks include limited operating histories, reliance on the advisors, conflicts of interests, payment of substantial fees to the advisors and their affiliates, illiquidity and liquidations at less than the original amounts invested." In other words, these kinds of alternative investments are not for everyone, thus the term, alternative. The share redemption plans of non-traded investments are limited and subject to suspension, modification or termination at any time. Additionally, redemptions, if they occur at all, can be at less than purchase price. Investors should consult a financial professional to determine whether risks associated with an investment in the shares are compatible with their investment objectives."

Benefits and Risks of Investing in a BDC

A BDC is a public offering, and thus must meet SEC requirements, but that doesn't imply endorsement.

As with traded BDCs, non-traded BDCs are regulated by federal securities laws including The Securities Act of 1933, the Securities Exchange Act of 1934, certain provisions of the Investment Company Act of 1940, and the Sarbanes-Oxley Act of 2002.

Non-traded BDCs must make regular SEC disclosures, including quarterly and annual financial reports, as required by the Securities Exchange Act of 1934, as amended. These reports are filed with the SEC and are publicly available.

Non-traded BDCs are also regulated by state securities laws, including guidelines established by the North American Securities Administrators Association.

Per the Investment Company Act of 1940, BDCs must value their portfolios on a regular basis.

DST - Delaware Statutory Trust Funds

Investment firms focused on energy-centric real asset strategies and investments. This investment gives opportunities throughout the energy value-chain to family offices and ultrahigh-net-worth individuals. Energy-centric real-asset focus include on shore E&P, midstream, and related infrastructure and services.

Want to jump in? You absolutely need a qualified Financial Advisor. But it's good to know something about these terms and acronyms.

11.

Risk Management - Insurance

When you start looking into insurance the first question to answer is: What is the purpose? Some of the answers are very obvious, others not so much.

Health

Implementing health care in the US has been a long 100 years of struggle. From the Roosevelts, Truman,

Eisenhower, Nixon, Kennedy, and Johnson, to Ford and Clinton, presidents have tried and failed to establish national health care. Until President Obama. On March 23, 2010, President Obama's administration finally passed a health reform initiative.

Since that health insurance law, 16.4 million Americans gained health insurance coverage. 129 million people who could have otherwise been denied or discriminated against now have access. For more information, see www.whitehouse.gov/health-care-in-america. Of course, by the time you read this, it all may change, which is not always good news.

When President Theodore Roosevelt campaigned for national health insurance in August 6, 1912, he stated that "There is also the problem of economic loss due to sickness-a very serious matter for many families with and without incomes, and therefore, an unfair burden upon the medical profession."

President Franklin D. Roosevelt introduced a bill for a comprehensive health reform and he commented, "Millions of our citizens do not now have a full measure of opportunity to achieve and enjoy good health. Millions do not now have protection or security against the economic effects of sickness. The time has arrived for action to help them attain that opportunity and that protection."

On January 31, 1955, President Truman detailed his

plan for a health care reform: "Many of our fellow Americans cannot afford to pay the costs of medical care when it is needed, and they are not protected by adequate health insurance. Too frequently the local hospitals, clinics, or nursing homes required for the prevention, diagnosis and treatment of diseases do not exist or are badly out of date."

On February 9, 1961, President Eisenhower commented on the high costs of health care and the need to fix it.

Each president in the last decade realized that the nation's health was important and that the system of health care in the US was a problem in need of solving. So, national health care was never a new idea. But it's important to know that we all now must have health insurance or pay a penalty.

Find a good insurance agent who will help you through the maze of questions needed to find the right health insurance for you.

Property & Casualty Insurances:

Auto Insurance

The second mandatory insurance is auto insurance. Most states in the US require auto insurance, and you can lose your license if you do not have proper coverage. The insurance should cover the value of your car, either to repair or replace. With luck, you will never earn back the payments for this insurance. But as is the case with Long Term Care insurance, you are paying a small monthly amount to hedge against risks and accidents. Driving without insurance is an enormous risk.

Insurance premiums for younger drivers are higher than for mature drivers. Companies have, not surprisingly, calculated the risks of auto accidents by age group. The younger you are, the more statistically accident prone. Your premiums will decrease after age 25. One way to keep your premium low is to sign up for a higher deductible. You do need to make sure you will have the deductible readily available. If your deductible is $1,000 or $500, you will need to be able to pay that amount when you pick up your car at the auto body shop.

Home Insurance

When you buy a home, you should calculate the cost of insuring this big asset. Home insurance is both prudent and often a requirement in order to secure the mortgage loan for the house. The mortgage company wants its asset protected. We know the expenses of owning a home sometimes seem overwhelming and might lead you to wonder whether you should add this extra expense. The answer is yes. Home insurance is not useless; it is essential.

Here's an example: You invite friends or family to a

lovely large party. One of your guest's trips on the back steps and breaks his ankle. You, as the homeowner, are potentially liable for the guest's injury. The right homeowner's insurance policy should protect you against legal action and should pay for the injured persons medical bills.

Now that you know why you need it, let's take a look at what it is you're buying.

Different policies exist for renters, owners of mobile homes, people seeking bare bones coverage, and those living in homes that are very old. Most homeowners will purchase what is called an HO-3 policy. This insurance policy covers your home and its contents against damage and theft, as well as you, the owner, against personal liability if someone is injured while on your property. This coverage also includes damage caused by pets and most major disasters (not that your pets are a disaster). Floods and earthquakes require separate policies. Homeowner's insurance does not cover problems that result from poor maintenance or general wear and tear on the property.

A basic homeowner's insurance policy should cover any other structures on your property and should cover living expenses in case you are not able to live at home after a fire or other insured disaster. The amount of coverage provided for each of these items varies depending on the insurer and the type of policy. Again, a good agent is very important. A Certified Financial Planner does not usually sell this product but is trained to give you a review of your property and insurance options.

Disability

Disability insurance protects your income if you become disabled.

According to Gallup's recent Economy and Personal Finance Poll, a majority of us would suffer severe financial hardship if we were unable to work for even a few months. That same poll reported Fourteen percent of US workers say that if they lost their jobs, they could only live for one week before experiencing significant financial hardship. Twenty-nine percent said they could live for one month. Twenty-six percent said they could last four months, while only about one-third of workers could get by for a year or more.

That's where disability insurance can come in - providing a way for you to help pay your bills while you're on the road to recovery.

If you become disabled and aren't able to work, disability insurance kicks in to cover part of your salary until you can return to your job. Disability insurance - whether it's through an employer or a policy you buy yourself - pays out a percentage of your income if you get sick or injured and can't work.

Short-term disability insurance typically covers you for three months, and long-term disability insurance kicks in after the short-term period ends. Long-term disability usually lasts for 2, 5, or 10 years, or until age 65 or 67, depending on the policy.

Generally, individual disability insurance replaces 45%-65% of your income. Disability insurance through work typically pays 60% of your income.

Who needs disability insurance? Anyone who has a job should consider purchasing disability insurance. Remember: your ability to earn income is your most valuable asset.

The nonprofit *Life Happens*, which helps educate consumers about insurance, says you have a 30% chance of having an illness or injury that keeps you out of work for 90 days or longer. In most cases, the disability isn't work-related, so you won't be able to collect workers' compensation.

Where can I get disability insurance?

You may be covered by a group disability insurance policy through your job or you might qualify for disability coverage through the Social Security Administration. You can also purchase an individual policy.

How much does disability insurance cost?

Similar to life insurance, the cost of disability insurance is tied to your age and health. If you're young and in good health, you'll typically pay less than someone who is older and has health issues.

If you have major health issues, you might not be able to purchase disability insurance or it might be prohibitively expensive.

Do I need more coverage if I have disability insurance through my job?

Most financial advisers say having an individual disability insurance policy in addition to what you have through work is a must. Plans offered through your employer often fall short of the coverage you will likely need.

Most disability plans through work pay you 60% of your salary, but you may not actually get that amount in benefits.

Typically, your employer pays the cost of coverage, but if you have to collect, you'll have to pay taxes on your insurance benefits, says John Nichols, president of the Disability Resource Group in Chicago.

And if you change jobs, you'll lose that particular coverage.

Do I need an individual policy if I can get coverage through Social Security?

You also may be eligible for Social Security coverage if you're judged to be totally disabled (see the Social Security Administration to determine this applies to you). But it can be hard to qualify for that coverage, and in 2017 the average payout was about $1,171 per month - far less than many people's monthly expenses.

What should I look for in an individual policy?

There's no one-size-fits-all solution if you're looking for an individual disability policy, so you should consider working with an insurance or financial adviser. There are plenty of variations, and you need to craft the policy that works best for your situation.

What are the terms I should know to understand disability insurance?

Partial or total disability coverage

Decide which scenario is best for you: a policy that only kicks in if you're totally disabled, or one that allows you to collect partial payment if you're partially disabled and can only work part-time.

Elimination period

This is the length of time you'll need to be out of work before collecting any payment. It's often 30, 60, or 90 days. A policy with a shorter elimination period costs more.

Benefit period

This is the length of time you'll collect your benefits. It could be for two years, five years, until age 65, until retirement age, or for another period of time.

Occupational class

The cost of coverage in part depends on your job. If you have a white-collar job, you'd generally pay less than a blue-collar worker.

Own occupation vs. any occupation

You can get coverage that takes effect if you can't do your particular profession or you can purchase a policy that covers you if you can't perform any occupation. Someone like a neurosurgeon might opt for coverage for their own profession. This coverage is more expensive. Coverage for "any occupation" means you can't perform any job for which you have the education and training. For more on this contact your state Insurance Commissioner.

Inflation protection

A cost-of-living adjustment rider, or policy add-on, that will increase your benefits to keep pace with inflation if you become disabled - say, for instance, you become permanently disabled and are unable to work at age 30. Imagine how inflation would erode the value of your benefits by the time you reached middle age. This rider is recommended for younger people and adds 15-25% to the cost of a policy. If you're nearing retirement, the extra cost probably isn't worth it.

Waiver of premium

With this feature, you don't have to pay the disability insurance premium while you are disabled and collecting benefits.

Extra coverage for severe disability

In addition to paying a percentage of your salary, a policy with a catastrophic rider pays additional money if you're unable to perform two out of the six "activities of daily living" or if you have a cognitive impairment. The six activities of daily living, as defined by the Federal Long-Term Care Insurance Program, are eating, bathing, dressing, toileting, continence, and transferring (such as moving from a wheelchair to bed). This rider adds about 10% to the cost of a disability policy.

Retirement savings protection

This feature replaces the contributions to retirement savings while you're disabled and unable to work. The Guardian's Retirement Protection Plus rider, for instance, pays 100% of what you normally set aside for retirement, as well as any employer matching contributions, into a trust. A trustee invests the benefits at your direction.

How do I collect disability?

Your physician will determine if you can no longer "perform the substantial duties of your job." You may be sent to a special doctor to corroborate the disability claim.

Long Term Care Insurance

This insurance has now become custodial care or personal care. Long-term care is the assistance needed over an extended period of time to manage, rather than cure, a chronic condition.

It's about keeping you at home as long as possible. Long-term care is not covered under health insurance policies, such as Medicare or Medicare supplemental policies. This kind of insurance maybe needed any time young or old.

When Christopher Reeves the actor who was famous for playing Superman, on May 27, 1995 was thrown off his horse while participating in an equestrian competition in Culpeper, Virginia at the age of 43 he was confined to a wheelchair and required a portable ventilator for the rest of his life. He lobbied on behalf of people with spinal_cord_injuries and for human embryonic stem cell research, founding the Christopher Reeve Foundation and co-founding the Reeve-Irvine Research. He also at the age of 43 needed long term care. He died October 10, 2004 at the age of 52.

Long-term care is primarily the assistance or supervision you may need when you are not able to do some of the basic Activities of Daily Living (ADLs) such as bathing, dressing, going to the toilet, or moving from a bed to a chair. You might need assistance with ADLs if you suffer from an injury like a broken hip, prolonged illness, a stroke or frailty. You may also need long term care because of mental deterioration, called "cognitive impairment" that can be caused by brain disorders such as Alzheimer's or a mental illness.

Contact a CFP® or a specialist with this kind of insurance someone that can assist you with long-term care planning.

How Much Does Long-Term Care Cost?

In 2016, the cost of care averaged $330 a day with an annual cost of $120,450. If you self-insure the cost for home care with dignity, you will pay $361,350 in three years. Alzheimer's care in skilled nursing homes is usually subject to the same fee structure as regular nursing home care. This differs from assisted living communities which typically charge 20% - 30% over their standard fees to care for an individual with Alzheimer's.

You can see this can quickly go through your assets. Instead, use someone else's money and get long-term care insurance or asset care using whole life insurance to help provide coverage for long term care.

There are three options:

1. Using personal savings

2. Counting on government programs (Medical-Medicaid)

3. Or purchasing private insurance

Using personal savings is the equivalent to self-insuring. Personal funds are at risk in order to cover the potential cost of care. The government Medicare pays on average 23 days of care under its nursing home benefit, and benefits are not available after 100 days.

The last option is private insurance. Some life insurance policies allow for the acceleration of death benefit to pay for long-term care expenses. Annuities can also provide protection for personal care without the need for a medical exam. There are also large deposit-based plans that essentially prepay expenses and return a portion of the premium if long-term care expenses are not needed.

However, the most direct and efficient insurance to protect against the risk is long-term care insurance.

Life Insurance

A lot of people hate life insurance, but it's a little money for a lot of protection.

What is the purpose of the life insurance? Who and what are you protecting? For one, your loved ones. Life insurance typically helps your surviving partner pay off the mortgage, pay for education, provide income, and can serve as a tax-free loan.

Term insurance

Term insurance is usually written for a period of time 5 years, 10 years, 15 years, 20 years, and 30 years. This is really a bet with the insurance company. The insurance company bets you will not die within the time of your contract, and you are betting you will die and collect. Most times the insurance company is right and people do run out of contract and insurance. Term insurance should only insure for a short period and then convert to universal or adjustable life which will last longer and has much more usage.

Whole Life Insurance Investopedia describes whole life insurance as a contract with premiums that include insurances and investments. The protection is throughout the insured's entire lifetime. The investment side allows the insured to borrow on the contract. There are many different kinds of whole life policies to choose from. One of the most common and oldest policies is the level premium insurance called ordinary life. In the insurance industry, it is also known as straight life insurance; continuous and traditional. The main thing to remember is if it has a cash value and if premiums are paid on time, it will take care of your family until death.

The features on this life insurance contract are the level (or fixed) periodic premiums. They are calculated under the assumption that the policy owner can continue to fulfill the contract throughout the duration of his or her life. The death benefit remains level throughout the lifetime of the contract. The insurance companies developed this model to keep the whole life contract premiums from ever changing, making the premiums affordable for as long as the policy owner decides to keep it.

The investment side of the whole life contract has the ability to accumulate cash values. These values help maintain the reserve the insurer needs to accumulate at the beginning of the policy's life, allowing enough money for the years to come. This policy adds interest earned and a reserve that helps protect the insured as they age. Without the interest and the reserve, the insurance would not have sufficient money to pay for the increasing mortality cost as the insured ages. The cash value also gives the policy owner the ability to borrow money for any reason at any time, and it is usually not a taxable event. Surrendering the contract may cause a taxable event. Before surrendering your policy, consult with your insurance agent, tax specialist, or Financial Planner.

This policy will protect the insured for the rest of their lives (generally only to the age of 95 and at the most 100). The insurance company agrees to pay a fixed death payment when the insured dies if the owner of the policy has paid all the premiums. When you buy this policy and it has cash value, you have the right to surrender it for the cash value.

The most important reason for life insurance is to provide immediate estate cash when someone dies. The following are a few reasons for family protection:

To provide income for your dependent family until they can provide for themselves.

To pay off consumer, business, or mortgage debt.

To provide for your children's education and to pay for college or other training.

To pay for federal estate and state taxes, funeral expenses, and administration costs.

To help the family deal with the sale and continuation of a business through a "buy-sell" agreement.

To insure a business when a key employee is lost.

To protect a company by providing cash to help recruit, retain, retire, or reward one or more key employees through a salary continuation plan.

To refinance the company's debt and obligations, and to help the dependents of the deceased key employees.

To fund gifts for children, grandchildren, or others without the loss from expenses caused by probate costs, inheritance taxes, income taxes, federal estate taxes, transfer fees, or the generation-skipping transfer taxes.

To fund your favorite charity.

To avoid probate. Probate can be slow and costly. It can take up to three years for the courts to finally distribute an estate and in the process, the courts can take up to 10% of the estate to cover court and attorney fees. In the case of insurance, the amounts are not public and is therefore totally confidential. The only time it becomes public record is if the insurance beneficiary is the estate. Because it is given to a beneficiary and it is not public record, anyone can be a beneficiary.

The life insurance proceeds provide instant, untaxable cash within days of claiming to all dependents.

To better direct gamily assets through life insurance since it is not taxable and does not go through probate limiting state, local and federal taxes.

Whole life attributes

The best insurance for split dollar arrangements is the level premium whole life insurance. Split dollar life insurance is a strategy arrangement and is not an insurance product and not enough of a reason to buy insurance on its own. The strategy allows the sharing of cost and benefits of any permanent life insurance policy. For an executive of the company to have the company pay for the life insurance and should the executive die the insurance will pay the company.

A good reason for a split dollar plan is it's not subject to ERISA (Employee Retirement Income Security Act of 1974) rules. This allows a lot of flexibility in how the agreement is written. This contract does require a close look at other laws so a good, qualified attorney and tax specialist should be consulted as you draw up the contract.

Corporations may want to use the level premium whole life to finance post-retirement health insurance, since it is a tax-sheltered way to finance for a selected group of executives and key employees. Additionally, the cash from the policy can be used for health insurance premium payments for retirees. The corporation receives the death proceeds free from federal income tax when the employee dies (alternative minimum tax liability may be the exception). This helps the corporation receive reimbursement for part or all of the costs accrued while providing post-retirement health insurance. Corporate Owned Life Insurance (COLI) may be another way to recover post-retirement health insurance liabilities.

The advantages of whole life insurance

The annual premium is fixed and known. Participating policies (policies that receive dividend payments from life insurance) will decline over the years due to the fixed premiums minus dividends.

There is a guaranteed ceiling on the mortality expense charges and a guaranteed floor on interest credited to the cash value of the policy.

During the lifetime of the insured or upon death, the cash value earnings accumulate tax-free or with taxes deferred depending on whether gains are distributed at death or surrendered during the life of the insured.

Tax-free municipal bonds pay less than ordinary life, through the combination of guaranteed cash values and dividend formulas, and they frequently pay higher effective interest on cash values.

The cash value has a very low market risk compared to longer term municipal bonds and other longer term fixed income investments. They do, however, have a higher market risk.

The policy owner can borrow on the cash value,

although they must pay interest on the policy loan. Whether or not the loan is repaid, the cash value does continue to grow. Borrowing on the policy is actually less than the stated policy value or loan rate.

Life insurance proceeds are not part of the probate estate, unless the estate is named as the beneficiary of the policy. Therefore, the beneficiary can receive the proceeds without the expense, delay, or uncertainty caused by administration of the estate.

No public record of the death benefit and to whom it is paid out.

Federal income taxes on proceeds is not usually taxable depending on the circumstances of the beneficiary relationship.

The insurance death benefit may be exempt from state inheritance taxes unless payable to the estate.

In some cases policy owners can use life insurance policies as collateral or security for personal loans.

The disadvantages of whole life insurance

Distributions of lifetime on the cash values may be taxable when the policy's extended cash value is more than the premiums paid. This creates a gain in the policy.

If you have limited financial resources, the premium

may be unaffordable.

The premium spent is usually higher in the early years since the payments are much higher than; however, when you hold the policy a long time the premiums become less expensive and will never run out.

If you surrender the policy within the first 5 to 10 years, this may result in a substantial loss because the surrender values will calculate the recovery of the sales commissions and the expense of the insurance company.

When borrowing on the insurance, the owners cannot deduct interest paid on policy loans on their tax returns as this is considered personal loans.

Because this is a long-term contract, the guaranteed return on this kind of insurance does not provide inflation protection. The dividends paid on some participating policies may be able to hedge against inflation. Hedging against inflation is limited to policies that reflect on favorable mortality.

Overall the rate of return from the cash value on a whole life contract is very competitive on a before tax comparison with alternative investments. Whole life may be a way to do as well as an alternative investment. Whole life is competitive because it has dividends and has guaranteed payments.

General Tax Rules

Life insurance death benefits are the only investment product left that is free of any federal and state income tax. The death benefits paid under these policies may be subject to the estate, gift, and generation-skipping transfer rules of taxation.

Taxation of living proceeds

Living proceeds from life insurance is covered under code Section 72 of the Internal Revenue Code. When you receive payments during the insured's life, the tax code separates the payments into three categories: 1) annuity payments, (2) payments of interest only, and (3) amounts not received as an annuity.

Annuity payments

Annuities are payments received from a contract that will systematically liquidate the contract. The Internal Revenue Code section 72 controls what portion of each payment is treated as a tax-free recovery of investment and what portion is treated as taxable income or gain. Each payment is considered part of the investment or the income and gain of this contract. Payments received are treated partially as recovery of investment and partially as taxable income until the entire investment has been recovered. Once the contract has been recovered, the payments thereafter are taxable income.

Payments of interest only

Payments consisting of interest only (i.e. they are not part of the systematic liquidation of a principal sum) are not annuity payments and are not taxed under the annuity rules. The living benefits are held by the insurance company under an agreement to pay interest; the interest payments are taxable in full when distributed.

Amounts not received as an annuity

In general, all living proceeds except for interest and annuity settlements are taxed under the "cost recovery rule." The categories are policy dividends, lump-sum cash settlements of cash surrender values, cash withdrawals, and amounts received on partial surrender. These are included in gross income only to the extent that they exceed the investment in the contract (as reduced by any prior excludable distributions received from the contract). The annuity distribution during life are first treated as a return of the owner's investments and then as a taxable interest or gain.

As to all investments, there are exceptions to this rule. The first exception is policies that initially fail the seven-pay test under the Modified Endowment Contract (MEC) rules. Because level premium policies are designed to have premiums payable for the life of the insured, they are not likely to fail the seven-pay test.

The second exception is when a policy originally satisfies the tests for MEC Treatment but, for some reason, changes in the benefits of the contract makes the policy fail the test.

Usually the ordinary level premium will not jeopardize the favorable MEC status. Limited pay policies and universal life are more likely to trigger the MEC. When an insurance contract is treated as a MEC, cash distribution becomes taxable under the interest-first rule. The rule states that distributions are first attributed to interest or gain in the contract and are fully taxable. After the interest or gain is exhausted, the distributions are treated as a nontaxable recovery of investment in the contract.

Loan proceeds

Policy loans under non-MEC life insurance policies are not treated as distributions. Policy loans, if still outstanding when surrendered, will be taxable on the borrowed amount to the extent the cash value exceeds the policy owner's premiums in the contract. Loans are paid off at the time of surrender.

Alternatives to whole life insurance

There is no alternative or substitute for life insurance because it provides an immediate estate when someone dies. Life insurance policies can provide tax-free cash benefits on death as well. The rare feature of level premium life insurance is the fact it is affordable. It provides lifetime coverage at the lowest level annual cost compared to other types of whole life policies. As a spin-off of level premium financing, the policy has a tax-free or tax deferred cash buildup.

A universal life policy configured as a level premium policy

A universal life policy can be initially constructed to resemble a level premium life policy. Unlike "true" level premium life policies, a universal life policy charges for mortality, and expenses can change in the universal life policy in a way that the policy owner would need to pay additional premiums in the future to maintain the death benefit coverage.

Premiums are set by life insurance companies who are free to set premiums according to their strategies. Almost all states have statutes prohibiting any form of rebating (i.e. sharing the commission with the purchaser) by the agent. The premium includes a "loading" fee to cover such things as commissions to agents, premium taxes payable to the state government, and operating expenses of the insurance company such as rent, mortgage payments and salaries.

Some companies offer "no-load" or "low-load" life insurance policies. There is not a no-load policy, because certain expenses are unavoidable (e.g. the premium tax), but some pay either no sales commission or a very low sales commission. These make it possible for the cash value to buildup and will make it larger in the beginning of the contract. No load has lower commission payouts, and they must spend more money on marketing and will also have higher administrative expenses.

The majority of expenses in a policy are during the period of time the policy is first issued. The insurance company may take 5 years or longer to recover from the cost of issuing a policy. An ongoing expense, that averages 2% of each premium payment, is the state premium tax. The first-year premium goes to the selling agent as commission paid. It will take 3 to 9 years to pay the agent, and about half the premium is payable in the year of sale and the other half is paid on a renewal basis.

When you have an ordinary level premium life insurance policy, there is no exact surrender charge. The participating policies usually will pay a terminal dividend. If you keep your policy for a long time, the terminal dividend is typically higher. This is a way for the insurance company to reward the policyholders who keep their policies longer.

Comparing Whole life and Universal Life

There are two common types of permanent life insurance policies: whole life and universal life. Deciding the difference between them can be difficult.

Both provide a financial benefit when someone dies. How to decide which policy is the best for you? When comparing the policies, consider: do they both offer cash value that may increase over time? Which one is more expensive or are they the same? What main differences excites between whole life insurance and universal life insurance?

Both policies are considered permanent policies. They were created to last your entire life, and as long as premiums are paid, they will not expire. They both accumulate cash value over time, and the owner is able to borrow against the policy tax-free, for any reason. Premiums are usually higher because of the ability to have cash value and the benefit of borrowing not provided with term insurance. Because of these benefits, premiums are usually higher with these policies.

Whole Life Insurance

The defining feature of this policy is the fixed premium; this is a premium that once established never changes. Like universal life insurance, it has the ability to accumulate cash value over time, making it possible to borrow the value with no need to pay it back until the policy is claimed at death and paid out. For example, if you have a face value policy of $100,000 and you borrowed $10,000 the payout at death would be $90,000 paying back the money you borrowed.

The whole life insurance policy provides life protection and insurance protection with an accumulation. This may be a good choice if you want a policy that gives you:

Level premiums that stay the same for the life of the policy

An accumulation of cash value that can be used while you're still alive

Protection you cannot outlive as long as you make your required premiums.

Universal Life Insurance

This policy allows you to skip payments when there is enough value accumulated. It adjusts the premiums up or down. You must make the minimum premium.

Because of the adjustable premium, the growth of the policy will depend on whether you add to your premium or you make the policy pay for itself. The minimum interest credited to the policy is established when you buy the policy. The insurance company, if it earns more than the minimum interest rate, may credit the policy with the excess interest.

This policy may be a good choice if you want:

Flexible and adjustable premiums.

The ability to borrow the cash value while you are still alive.

Permanent insurance. Including multiple payment options, the growth and cash you have earned over time to be tax-deferrable.

Special benefits including, the flexibility to change your death benefits while still giving you the potential to accumulate cash value over the time of the policy.

You may be able to get the policy to pay for itself by using the cash value to pay for the premiums and have no need to pay another premium due to the cash value. Caution: you need to make sure the cash value will be enough to start this strategy. Depending on the policy you may be allowed to increase or decrease the death benefit depending your circumstance.

Main Differences Between Whole and Universal Life Insurance

Universal life insurance has more flexible premiums than whole life. The premiums for the universal life insurance usually are lower during periods of high interest rates than whole life insurance premiums for the same coverage.

The interest on whole life is adjusted annually while universal life insurance is adjusted monthly. During the periods of rising interest rates, universal life insurance policy owners may see cash values increase at a rapid rate compared to those in whole life insurance policies.

It may be preferred to have set death benefits, level premiums, and the possibility of growth in a whole life insurance. Nevertheless, you may prefer to have flexibility and options which makes universal life more attractive.

Adjustable Life, according to Investopedia

Adjustable life insurance is also known as "flexible premium adjustable life insurance." It differs from other life insurance products in that there is no requirement to cancel or purchase additional policies as the insured's circumstances change. Adjustable life insurance policies are best suited for individuals who want the protection and cash value benefits of whole life insurance along with an increased measure of flexibility. With the ability to modify premium payments and face amounts, policyholders can customize their coverage as their income and indebtedness change through the years.

Adjustable life insurance can apply to certain policy types, such as universal life insurance and variable universal life insurance.

Commercial Insurance

This is the first insurance you should contemplate when you start a new business.

Regardless if you are starting as a new business owner, or have owned a business for many years, commercial insurance could stand as one of the most important financial investments to make in protecting the existence of your company.

Operating a business is extremely challenging without having to worry about suffering significant financial loss due to unforeseen circumstances. Commercial insurance can protect you from some of the most common losses experienced by business owners such as property damage, business interruption, theft, liability, and worker injury. Purchasing the appropriate commercial insurance coverage can make the difference between going out of business after a severe loss or recovering with minimal business interruption and financial impairment to your company's operations.

Buying Commercial Insurance

One of the first steps in purchasing small business insurance is to contact a licensed insurance broker-agent who specializes in commercial coverages. Beginning a working relationship with a reliable, competent broker-agent can be as crucial to your business plan as getting professional advice from an accountant, banker, human resources analyst, payroll specialist, lawyer, or a trusted business mentor.

Business contacts that you have made are excellent referral sources for recommending a broker-agent, especially if the contacts are in the same industry as your business or in a closely related industry.

Brokers and Agents

When looking for your broker-agent, it is important to verify the broker-agent's insurance license with the State Department of Insurance. The State Department of Insurance is responsible for licensing all broker-agents who sell or market insurance. A broker-agent is issued a fire and casualty license, which enables him/her to sell commercial property and casualty insurance. Fire and casualty broker-agents are required to follow state laws and codes, and to prominently display their license in the office. They may also be required to prominently print their license number on all business cards, written price quotations for insurance products, and print advertisements for insurance products distributed.

After you have interviewed several broker-agents and checked their license status with your state insurance licensing authority, you will be better able to determine the broker-agents with whom you would like to do business. While the term "broker-agent" is a specific license designation with the state licenser, brokers and agents act in different ways to secure insurance for consumers. Brokers may sell for many insurance companies and are usually paid by you in the form of a broker fee.

Agents are appointed by insurance companies and are paid a commission by the insurance company. It is possible to approach several agents for quotes on your commercial insurance business since any particular agent may represent a limited number of insurance companies.

Initially a broker-agent will meet with you to discuss your business operations and the exposures (the possibility of loss) that are specific for your industry and business type. If you currently have business insurance, the broker-agent will ask to review your current policy. This is a standard practice used to determine the current coverage you have. The broker-agent is comparing limits, exposure bases, business classifications, exclusions, and endorsements in order to analyze any gaps, errors, or overlaps that may exist in your current commercial policy.

It is not necessary to share the premiums you have paid for your current or prior business insurance, but you should be forthcoming with any other information that affects your business operations. The more credible information you provide to the broker-agent in the application process, the better the broker-agent can assess specific insurance needs and provide you with the best options to satisfy those needs and protect your business from loss.

Business Insurance

Depending on the individual risk characteristics of your business, the broker-agent will present you with different coverage options for purchasing commercial insurance. A broker-agent's proposal is just that, a proposal. When all is said and done, it is your responsibility to make an informed decision and to choose the insurance that best fits your business plan.

The relationship that you build with a broker-agent is extremely valuable in this critical decision-making process. An experienced broker-agent has dealt with hundreds of businesses similar to yours. Since commercial insurance can be complicated, you should feel free to discuss any terms, conditions, or concepts that are unclear to you with your broker-agent. It is part of a broker-agent's service to answer your questions and help you understand the insurance you are purchasing.

While your business may not need all commercial coverage lines, it is a good idea to have a basic knowledge of the types of insurance coverage available. As your business changes and expands, you will have the necessary knowledge to purchase insurance coverage as new exposures arise. The following commercial lines of insurance cover broad areas of exposure common to most business operations:

Property Insurance

Commercial insurance is divided into two main categories: property insurance and casualty insurance.

Property insurance provides coverage for property that is stolen, damaged, or destroyed by a covered peril. The term "property insurance" includes many lines of available insurance. Commercial Property, Inland Marine, Boiler and Machinery, and Crime are the four most common commercial property coverage lines. Each of these four property coverage lines is described below.

1. Commercial Property: Coverage Sections, Limits of Insurance, and Coinsurance

Buildings you own or lease as a part of your business, your Business Personal Property, and the Personal Property of Others make up the basic coverage sections of commercial property insurance. Commercial property insurance can be sold separately as an individual line policy (referred to as a monoline policy), or it can be sold as part of a Commercial Package Policy (CPP), which combines two or more commercial coverage parts such as commercial property, general liability, and commercial auto.

Building coverage includes buildings or structures and

any completed additions, which are listed on the declarations page of a commercial policy. The limit of insurance is the estimated amount needed to rebuild your building and to replace permanently installed fixtures, machinery, and equipment in the event of a total loss.

You are required under the insurance policy to fully insure the value of your buildings. If a building is not insured to value, you can be subject to a monetary penalty at the time of a loss. This penalty is commonly referred to as "coinsurance." It is important to read and understand the coinsurance clause of your commercial property policy and to discuss any questions with your broker-agent.

Business Personal Property consists of furniture; fixtures, machinery, and equipment not permanently installed; inventory; or any other personal property owned by and used in your business.

Personal Property of Others refers to property that is in your business's care, custody, and control. The type of business you operate will determine if you need to protect the personal property of others.

Covered Causes of Loss

Whether or not a property loss is covered depends upon the policy language, exclusions, and endorsements. You can choose the covered causes of loss in your property policy. Causes of loss are divided into two main categories: specified perils and open perils.

Specified Perils consist of a list of each peril to be insured against, such as fire, explosion, windstorm, vandalism, et cetera. You can usually request basic specified perils or broad specified perils coverage. Broad specified perils coverage adds to the list of covered perils found under basic specified perils.

Open Perils coverage covers all losses unless they are specifically excluded. Earth movement (including earthquake) and flood are two common perils that are excluded under open perils coverage. Since open perils coverage offers more comprehensive protection, it is costlier than a specified perils policy.

Valuation Types

Commercial property coverage will include a provision to determine what valuation method is to be used to pay the loss. The most common policy valuation method is Actual Cash Value (ACV). Unless otherwise defined in the policy, ACV is considered to be Fair Market Value in California.

There are two other methods of property valuation: agreed value and replacement cost. Agreed value waives any coinsurance penalty and pays 100% of the stated amount (agreed upon amount) for any covered loss. Replacement cost covers the amount it takes to replace your property with new property of like kind and quality up to the limits of insurance. Like ACV, replacement cost is subject to coinsurance.

Coverage Forms and Endorsements

There are various coverage forms and endorsements in addition to the basic property coverages already discussed that can customize coverage in a commercial property insurance policy. The following are the most common coverage forms and endorsements used in commercial property insurance:

Builder's Risk

Covers a new building or structure under construction, or an existing structure undergoing additions, alterations, or repairs. It is added to a policy for a minimum one-year term. Cancellation is allowed on a pro rata basis upon project completion; however, midterm cancellation will result in a short rate penalty.

A reporting form or renovations form allows coverage to be carried according to the stage of completion (i.e. as more of the project is completed, more value is reported, resulting in the proper amount of coverage for each stage of construction).

Legal Liability or Fire Legal Liability

Covers your legal liability for loss or damage to real and personal property of others as the result of your negligent acts and/or omissions. The loss or damage must be caused by a covered peril (including loss of use). The loss must be accidental and the coverage most often is purchased for tenants in commercial buildings.

Building Ordinance or Law

Provides coverage if the enforcement of any building, zoning, or land-use law results in loss to the undamaged portion of the building (Coverage A); demolition and removal costs of undamaged parts of the structure (Coverage B); or any increased cost of repairs or reconstruction (Coverage C). Replacement cost must be in effect for Coverage C to be applied.

Improvements and Betterments

Covers all permanently installed improvements and betterments, which cannot be removed when a tenant vacates the building. Usually added by a lienholder.

Glass

Basic specified perils for glass coverage include any resulting damage to other property from broken glass due to vandalism as well as vandalism to glass building blocks. Broad and specified perils cover $100 per pane of glass (up to $500 per occurrence). A glass form must be added for scheduled glass coverage when there is a significant glass exposure to insure. The glass form includes the number of panes, dimensions, location, lettering, and ornamentation. A separate glass deductible may be scheduled as well.

Peak Season

An endorsement that provides additional limits on personal property inventory during a designated period of time. This is specifically used to cover fluctuating inventory values before and during peak shopping seasons.

Inflation Guard

Automatically adjusts the limits of insurance to keep up with inflation. The adjustment can be tied to the construction cost index in a regional area or a specified percentage per year. This endorsement can be very important in helping to maintain adequate coverage limits, which can protect against potential coinsurance penalties in a property loss.

Time Element

Covers other losses stemming from a direct loss by a covered peril to business property. Business interruption, extra expense, and loss of rents and rental value are the most common time element coverages. Business interruption coverage replaces lost business income after a covered loss. Certain key employees can be named, allowing the employer to continue to pay their salaries until the business restarts operations after a loss. Extra expense coverage mainly applies to service or product related companies where the business must continue to ensure the survival of the company. Extra expense can pay for office space, equipment rental, advertising, or most costs considered reasonable for keeping the company operating after a covered loss.

Loss of rents and rental value

Covers loss of rental income caused by damage or destruction of a building rendering it unfit for occupancy.

2. Inland Marine

Without prior knowledge of inland marine insurance, it is easy to assume that this insurance line has something to do with boating transportation. In fact, inland marine insurance can cover a variety of transportation exposures; however, it does not cover boating transportation, which is covered under ocean marine insurance.

Inland marine is a specialized type of property insurance that primarily covers damage to or destruction of your business property while in transport. Inland marine also covers the liability exposure for the damage or destruction that may occur to property in your care, custody, or control during transport.

Covered Causes of Loss

Standard perils may include fire, lightning, windstorm, flood, earthquake, landslide, theft, collision, derailment, overturn of the transporting vehicle, and bridge collapse.

Coverage Forms and/or Specialty Coverages

Inland marine has great flexibility in covering many potential transportation risks. Some of the most common types of coverage offered are accounts receivable insurance, consignment insurance, equipment floaters (i.e. contractor's equipment), installation floaters, motor truck cargo insurance, trip transit insurance, and valuable papers (records) insurance. If you have questions regarding particular business, then contact your broker-agent for further information.

3. Boiler and Machinery

Boiler and machinery insurance can add an important layer to potential insurance coverage. Boiler and machinery insurance is currently marketed under such names as "systems protector," "systems breakdown," and "machinery breakdown" insurance. Boiler and machinery insurance covers business property, other property losses, and legal fees (if any) that may result from the malfunction of boilers and machinery. Boiler coverage includes covering the costs of inspection and often the maintenance of boilers, too.

Machinery coverage can include many different types of machines used in retail, office, and manufacturing settings. Machinery coverage also includes major machinery systems common to most commercial buildings, such as heating, ventilating, and air conditioning systems. Since most commercial property policies exclude losses from boilers and machinery, it is important to be aware of any exposure your business may have and discuss it with your broker-agent.

4. Crime

Crime insurance provides protection for the assets of your business including merchandise for sale, real property, money, and securities. It is considered a property insurance line. Based on the crime coverage that you purchase, it is possible to be covered for the following causes of loss: robbery, burglary, larceny, forgery, and embezzlement. Specialty coverage parts can be added based on need and exposure to loss such as mercantile open-stock, burglary insurance, mercantile robbery insurance, mercantile safe burglary insurance, money and securities broad form policy, office burglary and robbery insurance, and storekeeper's burglary and robbery insurance.

Casualty Insurance

Casualty Insurance provides coverage primarily for the

liability from the negligent acts and omissions of an individual, business, or organization that causes bodily injury and/or property damage to a third party. Commercial Automobile, Commercial General Liability, Commercial Umbrella, and Workers Compensation are the four most common business casualty insurance lines. (For more insurance terms, just in case you can't get enough, check out - http://www.naic.org/consumer)

1. Commercial Automobile

Coverage, Classification and Limits of Insurance

Commercial automobile coverage is similar to the coverage you may carry on your personal auto; however, commercial automobile exposures can be more complex requiring specialty coverages to be considered based on the individual needs of your business.

Basically, commercial automobile coverage can protect your company from any liability stemming from automobiles used in your business or any damage to the covered automobile. A Business Auto Policy (BAP) has the flexibility to provide coverage for business, personal, non-owned, or hired autos based on the coverage purchased and applied to each scheduled auto. In other words, automobiles can be separately scheduled along with corresponding coverages.

Coverage can differ by vehicle, and symbols will designate the coverage assigned to a scheduled auto. These symbols are referred to as covered auto symbols and use a simple numerical system (1-13). The automobiles are classified by weight (light, medium, heavy, extra heavy) and by type of use (private passenger, service, commercial).

Unlike personal auto policies that separate bodily injury and property damage limits (split limits), BAPs commonly utilize a Combined Single Limit (CSL) for the limit of insurance. This creates higher limits for both coverages, including per occurrence limits. Common commercial automobile CSLs are $500,000 or $1,000,000.

2. Commercial General Liability

Coverage

One of the key concepts of liability coverage is that it is comprehensive in nature. What this means is that the policy (insuring agreement) covers all hazards within the scope of the insuring agreement that are not otherwise excluded.

It is likewise comprehensive in that it provides automatic coverage for new locations and activities of your business, which come about after policy inception and throughout the policy term. Commercial General Liability (CGL) is the standard commercial liability policy used to insure businesses.

There are three primary coverage sections that make up a CGL policy: Premises Liability, Products Liability, and Completed Operations.

Premises Liability covers liability for accidental injury or property damage that results from either a condition on your premises or your operations in progress, whether on or away from your premises.

A Products Liability hazard exists for any business that manufactures, sells, handles, or distributes goods or products. The hazard is the potential liability for bodily injury or property damage that arises out of your products.

Completed Operations covers your potential liability for bodily injury or property damage that arises out of your completed work.

The major exclusions under a CGL policy include: intentional injury; insured contracts; liquor liability; worker's compensation and employer's liability; pollution; aircraft; automobile; watercraft; mobile equipment; war; care, custody, and control; damage to your work; impaired property; sister ship liability; and failure to perform.

It is always important to read and understand all coverage exclusions; however, it is particularly critical in a liability policy. If you do not understand the coverage exclusions or limitations of the CGL policy, then contact your broker-agent and discuss completely until a working understanding is achieved.

Classification

The type of business you run determines how a CGL policy is classified. Generally speaking, a specific code (or codes in some situations) is assigned based on exposures that are common to your type of business operation.

The first step in determining premiums is to classify the business risk, an important part of the rating formula. Obviously, this project is not for the faint of heart. Like most of the information in this chapter, seek out professional advice, I wanted to give you an idea of what is necessary and what many business owners forget to do!

Limits of Insurance

The CGL policy has separate limits of insurance for general liability, fire legal liability, products and completed operations liability, advertising and personal liability, and medical payments. An aggregate limit of liability is used for the general liability, fire legal liability, advertising and personal liability, and medical payments claims.

When total claims for all these areas exceed a stated annual aggregate limit of liability, the policy limits are exhausted and no more claims will be paid from the policy for the duration of the policy period. There is also a separate aggregate limit of liability in force for products and completed operations liability claims.

3. Commercial Umbrella

When a liability claim goes above the aggregate limit of liability, the policy limits are exhausted. By purchasing a commercial umbrella, you can protect your business from being liable for this excess liability judgment.

A commercial umbrella covers the amount of loss above the limits of a basic liability policy. Commercial automobile, CGL, worker's compensation, or any liability policy can be covered by a commercial umbrella. A commercial umbrella may also provide coverage if a basic liability policy is not in force. Also, commercial umbrellas can provide coverage for gaps in coverage under basic liability policies.

When a commercial umbrella provides coverage for basic liability loss, it does not pay the loss from the first dollar. It is common to have a Self-Insured Retention (SIR) amount of at least $10,000. SIR is similar to a deductible. If there is a commercial umbrella loss and there is no corresponding underlying policy in force, you must pay the first $10,000 of the loss before the umbrella policy responds.

4. Workers Compensation

When an employee suffers a work-related injury or illness, worker's compensation insurance steps in to provide benefits based on the type of illness or injury sustained. Workers compensation is based on a no-fault system, which means that an injured employee does not need to prove that the injury or illness was someone else's fault in order to receive worker's compensation benefits for an on-the-job injury or illness.

You must obtain a certificate from the California Department of Industrial Relations, Office of Self-Insurance Plans. Private employers have to post security as a condition of receiving a certificate of consent to self-insure. Self-insurance is only a viable option for very large, stable employer's due to the large amounts of security required to be posted.

For complete information on worker's compensation self-insurance, contact the California Department of Industrial Relations, Office of Self-Insurance Plans. See the "Resources" section for contact information.

Coverage Sections

Workers compensation insurance is divided into two coverage sections. In part one, the insurance company agrees to promptly pay all benefits and compensation due to an injured worker by worker's compensation laws of the states listed on the declarations page of the policy.

In part two, the employer is protected against situations where an employee can sue for injuries suffered under common law liability (i.e. consequential bodily injury, loss of consortium, dual capacity, or third party over actions). These types of injuries in the course of employment are not covered under worker's compensation law and are therefore not compensable under the worker's compensation part one.

Classification and Rating

Classification of worker's compensation insurance is based upon the specific duties that your employees perform in the course of their employment with your company. These classifications are developed and assigned by the Workers Compensation Insurance Rating Bureau (WCIRB) in most cases.

Business Insurance

Designed specifically for small businesses, a Business Owners Policy (BOP) is a combination commercial policy that covers property, general liability, and business interruption. It is written with strict underwriting guidelines including maximum allow-able square footage for office, retail, or apartment risks. A BOP is most appropriate for small, "main street" businesses such as hardware stores, barbershops, greeting card shops, accountant offices, or low-density apartment houses. Discuss the option of a BOP with your broker-agent, as the premium for qualifying businesses can be very competitive.

Rating a Policy

The way a policy is rated determines how the policy premium is developed. Rating factors vary based on the line of insurance you are purchasing. If you are purchasing commercial property insurance, the building rating formula is based on factors including square footage, type of construction, sprinkler red or non-sprinkler red (the sprinkler systems you may need to install), and the fire protection classification. If you are purchasing general liability insurance, the rating formula can be based on square footage, payroll, or gross sales depending on the classification codes used. These are known as rating exposures.

Once the rating exposures are identified and the deductibles selected (usually from information you have provided on the application), the premium is calculated by a simple formula: rate x exposure = premium. The deductible amount you choose will be calculated in the rate. The higher the deductible (the amount you choose to self-insure), the lower the rate.

By utilizing higher deductibles, you can bring your premium cost down; however, you do not want to jeopardize your company's financial future by choosing overly large deductibles. Speak with your broker-agent for the deductible options available to you when purchasing commercial insurance.

The basic rating equation most often utilizes other modification factors, which can include experience modifications, schedule rating, or judgment rating. Because rating formulas can range from simple to complex depending on the line of insurance, it is important to discuss how your policy is rated and how the policy premium is calculated with your broker-agent.

Deductible

The deductible on a commercial policy is the part of the loss that you pay up-front before your insurance company pays a claim. Based on the amount of the deductible as stated in your policy, the insurance company will pay up to the limits of the policy when a claim is covered after you have provided the deductible payment. The type of deductible utilized in a commercial policy is referred to as an "absolute dollar amount." The higher the absolute dollar amount (deductible), the lower your premium.

Loss Control

One of the most effective ways to decrease the frequency and potential severity of claims is through loss prevention and control. Most commercial insurance companies have their own loss prevention departments;

however, some insurers rely upon contracted loss prevention services. Usually loss control services are built into higher risk/higher premium accounts as a part of the insurance package.

If you are a small business owner, you can still benefit from proven loss control methods. Based on your type of business exposure, your broker-agent can offer suggestions on how to best control the loss exposures common to your business. The broker-agent, along with your account underwriter, claims representative, and loss control representative, can create an entire program of loss prevention that includes specific modifications and procedures to follow that can help create a safer workplace.

Surplus Line Insurance

The California FAIR Plan has been in operation since 1968 to provide basic property insurance to property owners who are unable to obtain insurance in the standard market. Although the California FAIR Plan was established by the legislature, it is not a state agency. It is an association of all property insurers licensed in the state, who participate according to the percentage of property insurance they write in California.

The majority of California FAIR Plan business is in designated urban, inner city, and areas subject to destructive wildfires. While the plan primarily writes policies for personal property holders (homeowners), they do write a small percentage of policies for commercial property owners. Any broker-agent can help you place a commercial property policy with the California FAIR Plan.

Cancellation and Nonrenewal

Commercial insurance companies must follow the rules set out in the insurance code regarding cancellation and nonrenewal. There are separate insurance code sections covering cancellation and nonrenewal for worker's compensation, auto, ocean marine, surplus line, reinsurance policies, and other commercial insurance lines. Contact your State insurance department.

Commercial insurance, by its very nature, is complex. However, it is possible with the assistance of a competent licensed broker-agent to steer clear of the pitfalls and make good decisions when purchasing insurance for your business.

Resources:

A.M. Best Company
A.M. Best Road
Oldwick, NJ 08858
Phone: 908-439-2200
Web Site:www.ambest.com

Moody's Investors Service
99 Church Street
New York, NY 10007
Phone: 212-553-0377
Web Site:www.moodys.com

Standard & Poor's
One Market Stuart Tower, Suite 1500
San Francisco, CA 94105
Phone: 415-371-5000
Web Site:www.standardandpoors.com

Weiss Ratings
15430 Endeavour Drive
Juniper, FL 33478
Phone: 800-289-9222
Web Site:www.weissratings.com

Western Insurance Agents Association (WIAA Group)
11190 Sun Center Drive, Suite 100
Rancho Cordova, CA 95670
Phone: 916-443-4221
Web Site:www.wiaagroup.org

Fitch Ratings
One State Street Plaza
New York, NY 10004
Phone: 212-908-0500 or 800-753-4824
Web Site:www.fitchratings.com

Workers Compensation Insurance Rating Bureau (WCIRB)
525 Market Street, Suite 800
San Francisco, CA 94105-2767
Phone: 888-229-2472
Web Site:www.wcirbonline.org
Policyholder Ombudsman Phone: 415-777-0777

Insurance Brokers and Agents of the West (IBA West)
7041 Koll Center Parkway, Suite 290
Pleasanton, CA 94566-4041
Phone: 800-772-8998Web
Site:www.ibawest.com

Insurance Glossary

Actual Cash Value - Unless otherwise defined in the policy, Actual Cash Value means Fair Market Value. The Fair Market Value of an item is the dollar amount that a knowledgeable buyer (under no unusual pressure) is willing to pay and a knowledgeable seller (under no unusual pressure) is willing to accept.

Agent - A licensed individual or organization authorized to sell and service insurance policies for an insurance company.

Aggregate Limit - The maximum dollar amount of coverage in force for a property damage policy or liability policy. This maximum amount can be figured on a per occurrence basis or as a general aggregate for the complete policy term.

Agreed Value - A method of loss valuation where the insured and the insurer list an agreed upon amount to be paid in case of loss. This valuation method is most common in property insurance when insuring valuable artwork, antiques, or classic autos. A professional appraisal is usually required.

Arbitration Clause - A clause in an insurance policy that allows the insured and the insurer to each appoint an arbitrator if they cannot agree upon an appropriate claim settlement. Once the arbitrators have been selected, they in turn appoint an independent umpire. If the arbitrators disagree, then the umpire decides which claims settlement to support. The final decision is binding.

Betterment - A situation that occurs in a loss when an old piece of property is replaced by a brand-new item. The insured is put in a better financial position than they were before the loss occurred, and consequentially may have to pay the difference in price for the betterment.

Binder - A short-term agreement that provides temporary insurance coverage until the policy can be issued or delivered.

Broker - A licensed individual or organization that sells and services insurance policies on your behalf.

Broker-Agent - A licensed individual who can act as an agent representing one or more insurers and also as a broker dealing with one or more insurers representing your interests.

Cancellation - The termination of an in-force insurance contract by either the insured or the insurer before its normal expiration date.

Claim - Notice to an insurance company that a loss has occurred that may be covered under the terms and conditions of the policy.

Claim Adjuster - The person who evaluates the damage caused by a covered loss and determines the amount to be paid under the policy terms.

Claims Made - A liability insurance policy where coverage applies to claims filed during the policy period no matter when the loss occurred subject to a retroactive inception date.

Coinsurance - An insurance clause that defines the amount of each loss that the company pays according to the amount of insurance carried, divided by the amount of insurance required. This basic formula relates to a contracted percentage of coverage that must be required to prevent a coinsurance penalty.

Combined Single Limit - When bodily injury liability and property damage liability is expressed as a single sum (limit) of coverage.

Commercial Lines - Insurance coverages for businesses, commercial institutions, and professional organizations, as contrasted with personal insurance.

Commission - A portion of the policy premium that is paid to an agent by the insurance company as compensation for the agent's work.

Concurrent Causation - Occurs when two or more perils cause a loss. When only one of these perils is covered by the insurance policy, the court generally rules that the entire loss is covered. Many insurance companies have reworded their policies to clarify that only a loss attributed to a covered peril is indeed covered.

Conditions - The portion of an insurance contract that sets forth the rights and duties of the insured and the insurer.

Consequential Bodily Injury - In Workers Compensation, special circumstances can arise when a work-related injury causes some sort of non-work, related injury. (Please see Loss of Consortium, Dual Capacity, and Third Party Over glossary definitions.)

Coverage - Protection that is provided under an insurance policy.

Declarations (DEC) Page - Usually the first page of an

insurance policy that contains the full legal name of the insurance company, the policy number, effective and expiration dates, premium payable, the amount and types of coverage, and the deductibles.

Deductible - The amount of the loss that the insured is responsible to pay before benefits from the insurance policy are payable.

Depreciation - The actual or accounting recognition of the decrease in value of property over a period of time according to a predetermined schedule.

Dual Capacity - In Workers Compensation, an employer may be liable two ways to an employee who incurs bodily injury on the job as a result of using a product or service produced by that employer. The employee is eligible for Workers Compensation benefits and may also sue the employer because of the defectiveness of the injuring product or service.

Earned Premium - The portion of the policy premium paid by the insured that has been allocated to the insurance company's loss experience, expenses, and profit year to date.

Endorsement - A written agreement that changes the terms of an insurance policy by adding or subtracting coverage.

Effective Date - The starting date of an insurance

policy (i.e. the date the policy goes in to force).

Exclusion - A contractual provision in an insurance policy that denies or restricts coverage for certain perils, persons, property, or locations.

Experience Modification - The adjustment of premium resulting from the use of experience rating. Experience Rating Plans reflect an insured's past loss experience (usually from the past three years) and uses this experience to modify and determine the premium for the current policy year.

Expiration Date - The termination date of coverage as indicated on an insurance policy.

First Party - The policyholder (i.e. the insured) in an insurance contract.

Flat Cancellation - Cancellation that takes place on the policy's effective date. No premium charge is made; however, other charges (i.e. service) may apply.

Fraud- An intentionally deceptive act committed to obtain an unfair or unlawful advantage. Fraud usually involves monetary gain.

Frequency - The number of times a loss occurs.

Hazard - A circumstance that increases the likelihood or potential severity of a loss.

Indemnity - Compensation for a loss in a property and casualty contract. The objective is to restore an insured to the same financial position after the loss that the insured had prior to the loss. In the most basic sense, indemnity is compensation for a loss.

Independent Adjuster - A person or organization that provides claim adjusting services to different insurers on a contract basis.

Insurable Interest - Any interest (most commonly ownership) that a person, company, or corporation has in a subject of insurance such as a business, building, or auto, which can be damaged and may cause the person, company, or corporation financial loss or other tangible deprivation. Generally, an insurable interest must be demonstrated when a policy is issued and must exist at the time of loss.

Insurance - A method of shifting risk from a person, business, or organization to an insurance company in exchange for the payment of premium. The insurance company commits to be responsible for covered losses.

Insured - The policyholder(s) entitled to coverage under an insurance policy.

Insurer - The insurance company who issues insurance and agrees to pay for losses and provide covered benefits.

Insuring Agreement - The portion of an insurance contract that describes what is covered. The insuring agreement usually states the perils insured against, the person(s) and/or property covered, the property locations, and the period of the contract.

Judgment Rating - A rating modification that is based on the underwriter's experience, best judgment, and analysis in classifying and underwriting a particular type of risk.

Lapse - The termination of a policy because of a failure to pay premium when due; applicable to property and casualty insurance.

Liability Insurance - Coverage for a policyholder's legal liability resulting from injuries to other persons or damage to their property.

License - A certificate of authority issued by the CDI to an insurer, agent, broker, or broker-agent to transact insurance business.

Limits of Insurance - The maximum amount of benefits the insurance company agrees to pay in the event of a loss.

Loss of Consortium - A potential situation in any bodily injury claim (including Workers Compensation claims) where a spouse contends that the bodily injury of their partner deprives them of the natural affection (spousal duties), help, and companionship of said spouse.

Loss Payable Clause - A provision that authorizes the insurer to make a loss payment to a person, company, or organization (loss payee) other than the insured. The loss payee must have an insurable interest (such as a lienholder for business personal property or a mortgagee on real property).

Managing General Agent (MGA) - An agent contractually authorized by an insurance company to manage all or part of the insurer's business activities. An MGA can manage the marketing, underwriting, policy issuance, premium collection, appointing and supervision of other agents, claims payments, and reinsurance negotiations of an insurance company.

Material Misrepresentation - A factual falsification made in such a manner that the insurance company would have refused to insure the risk if the truth had been known at policy issuance. A material misrepresentation gives an insurance company grounds to rescind a contract.

Misquote - An incorrect estimate of an insurance premium.

Nonpayment of Premium - Failure by the policyholder to pay the premium on a policy or pay the installment premium payments due on a policy.

Nonrenewal - The termination of an insurance policy on its normal expiration date.

Occurrence - A liability insurance policy that covers claims arising out of occurrences that take place during the policy period, regardless of when the claim is filed.

Peril - Cause of loss.

Personal Lines - Insurance written on the personal and real property of an individual (or individuals) to include such policies as homeowner's insurance and personal auto insurance, as contrasted with commercial lines.

Policy - A contract that states the rights and duties of the insurance company and the insured.

Premium - The monetary payment that an insured makes to an insurance company in exchange for the contract indemnifying the insured against potential loss. Simply put, this is the payment made by the insured to keep an insurance policy in effect.

Producer - A term used by the insurance industry to refer to agent, brokers, broker-agents, and solicitors.

Pro Rata Cancellation - A cancellation of a policy by an insurance company that returns the unearned premium to the policyholder (the portion of the premium for the remaining time period that the policy will not be in force).

Provisions - The statement of policy conditions in an insurance policy.

Public Adjuster - A licensed person or organization that represents the policyholder by contract in property damage claims negotiations with an insurance company.

Quotation - An estimate of the cost of insurance based on the information supplied to the agent, broker, broker-agent, or the insurance company.

Recision - The cancellation of an insurance policy back to its effective date resulting in a return of all premiums charged.

Regulations - Requirements developed by the CDI that implement laws passed by the legislature. Regulations go through a public comment process and must be approved by the state Office of Administrative Law.

Reinstatement - The restoration of a lapsed or canceled policy.

Renewal - The continuation of an insurance policy (i.e. offer of renewal) into a new term from the same insurance company that issued the existing policy.

Replacement Cost - The amount that it costs to replace lost or damaged property with new property of like kind or quality in the local market.

Schedule Rating - A method of pricing property and liability insurance. Schedule Rating uses debits and credits to modify a base rate figured by the special characteristics of the risk exposure. Insurers develop Schedule Rating because actuarial experience shows a direct relationship between certain physical characteristics and the possibility of loss. Most schedule rating plans must be filed and approved by the CDI.

Second Party - The insurance company in an insurance contract.

Self-Insured Retention (SIR) - The portion of a property or liability loss retained by a policyholder.

Severity - The size of a loss. Loss severity is used as a factor in establishing premium rates.

Short Rate Cancellation - A cancellation initiated at policyholder's request in which the premium returned is subject to an administrative penalty.

Sistership Liability - Exists when a manufacturer refuses to withdraw a product as ordered by a government agency or company management. Once a defective product has been identified and recalled, an insurance company excludes all other claims arising from the defective product due to the negligent failure of the company to take the product off the market.

Split Limits - The technique for expressing limits of

liability coverage under a particular insurance policy by stating separate limits for different types of claims growing out of a single event or combination of events. Coverage can be split per person, per occurrence, between bodily and property damage, or in other ways.

Subrogation - The process of recovering the amount of claim damages paid out to a policyholder from the legally liable party. When a company pursues the legally liable third party, they are required to include the policyholder's deductible in the recovery process.

Third Party - An individual other than the policyholder or the insurance company who has suffered a loss and may be able to collect compensation under the policy due to the negligent acts or omissions of the policyholder.

Third Party Over - The legal doctrine that involves an injured employee bringing suit against a third party who (for one reason or another) is able to bring an action against the employer.

Underwrite - The process to evaluate the insurance application and independent sources in order to verify the information provided and to determine the acceptability of the risk.

Underwriter - The person who performs the underwriting process to accept, reject, or modify risks on behalf of the insurer.

Unearned Premium - The premium corresponding to the time period remaining on an insurance policy. Unearned premiums are proportionate to the unexpired portion of the insurance and appear as a liability on the insurer's balance sheet, since they would be paid back upon cancellation of the policy.

For example, at the end of the first year of a fully prepaid five-year insurance policy with insurance premiums of $2,000 per year, the insurer has earned a premium of $2,000 and has an unearned premium of $8,000.

Waiver - The relinquishment of a known right, which may be expressed or implied.

Written Premium - The total premium on all policies written by an insurer during a specified period of time, regardless of what portion has been earn.

12.

Taxes and Tax Planning

As of 2016, the internal revenue code weighed in at 73,954 pages. It goes without saying that this level of complication requires a specialist. Using www.csea.org, find an EA in your local area. EA's or CPA's will help with all your tax issues.

A good time to start tax planning is October, November and December. Your tax professional can help you strategize and properly plan for the tax amount that may be owed by April 15th. Check in with your tax professional throughout the year especially if you are getting more earnings this year than the year before. If you have earned bonuses and commissions, you may be surprised at the end of the year.

If you receive a 1099 instead of a W-2, you may need to pay estimated taxes. Estimated taxes are required by self-employed businesses. If you owe more than $500 at the time of your return you may incur penalties. Remember before you do anything with money (e.g. make investments or acquire rental property), like investments, capital gains, earnings, sudden wealth and rental property, check with your tax professional so you know the taxes and costs. Benjamin Franklin said “It’s not what you make, it’s what you keep”.

Underpayment of Estimated Tax

Here is the direct language from irs.gov:

“If you did not pay enough tax throughout the year, either through withholding or by making estimated tax payments, you may have to pay a penalty for underpayment of estimated tax. Generally, most taxpayers will avoid this penalty if they owe less than $1,000 in tax after subtracting their withholdings and credits, or if they paid at least 90% of the tax for the current year, or 100% of the tax shown on the return for the prior year, whichever is smaller. There are special rules for farmers and fishermen. Please refer to *Publication 505, Tax Withholding and Estimated Tax,* for additional information."

Note: the publications on the IRS.gov website are just guides. For accurate and actionable information, check out the actual Federal Tax Law - *Internal Revenue Code (IRC), enacted by Congress in Title 26 of the United States Code (26 U.S.C.).*

The Beauty of Tax Credits

Let's talk about the beauty of a tax credits and how they are used. A tax credit is an actual deduction from your taxes. Let us say you owe $1,000; a tax credit of $1,000 makes your taxes zero. Terrific, no?

Now how do you get tax credits? You may have such low income that you qualify for the Earned Income Credit, also known as EIC. There are several hoops you must jump through before you can qualify for the EIC, and one of them is having a very low income.

You usually need to invest into an asset that provides the credit. The low housing income credit, energy credit, auto tax credit, oil and gas, and other types of credit investments may qualify. This kind of investment has risk, and you need to make sure you understand the risk before investing. Ask your CFP® if this is an appropriate investment for you.

Move to Non-Tax State

Taxpayers who are retired and earn taxable income from investments and retirement distributions can consider moving to a low-tax or no-tax state.

State income taxes vary greatly, from a top rate of 12.3% in California to zero in Alaska. Currently Alaska, Florida, Nevada, South Dakota, Texas, Washington, and Wyoming do not have an individual state income tax. Oftentimes, a person's choice of where to live has very little to do with state income tax rates.

Living close to family members, enjoying good weather, and employment opportunities may have a stronger influence on a person's choice of residence than state tax brackets. However, as family members move away and the taxpayer approaches the age of retirement, the desire to move to a no-tax state may become stronger. The moving to a non-tax state maybe worth considering if you research and make sure the state is not making up income tax with other types of taxation. All states need revenue.

Work in Foreign Countries

A taxpayer working in a foreign country may qualify to exclude a portion or all of his or her earnings from taxable income.

U.S. citizens and resident aliens who work outside the United States face a number of issues when filing personal tax returns. They are taxed on their worldwide income, regardless of the source of the income. Usually income earned in a foreign country is also taxed by that country, resulting in double taxation of the same income. The taxpayer may also have duplicate housing expenses or the value of employer-provided housing included in his or her income. Provisions exist for excluding part or all of foreign earned income, but understanding how to implement them is often problematic. Sometimes the tax return is due before the exclusion provisions can be met.

Worldwide income of U.S. citizens and resident aliens from all sources is subject to federal income tax, regardless of where the taxpayer is living. Filing requirements are independent of the taxpayer's residence. Compensation received in a foreign currency must be reported in U.S. dollars on the individual tax return. Foreign earned income is income that is earned while you are residing in a foreign country.

There are criteria for determining residence: either the bona fide residence test or the physical presence test. Foreign earned income can include U.S. source income received for work done in a foreign country. A foreign country does not include U.S. possessions, international waters, international airspace, or the continent of Antarctica. Airspace over a foreign country is considered part of the foreign country. U.S. citizens and resident aliens whose tax home is in a foreign country (other than Cuba or any other countries to which U.S. travel restrictions may apply at the time) and who have foreign earned income, may qualify for the following exclusions and deduction:

Exclusion from gross income of up to $101,300 earned income per individual for 2016. (visit the IRS web site, they are always happy to tell you the tax amount you owe) The exclusion is limited to the lesser of $100,800, or foreign earned income minus the foreign housing exclusion or deduction.

Exclusion from gross income of a limited amount of foreign housing expense paid with employer-provided amounts. Employer-provided amounts are any amounts that are taxable foreign earned income, including salaries, benefits, allowances, etc., and other amounts paid or incurred on the taxpayer's behalf, considered without regard to the foreign earned income exclusion.

Deduction, taken as an adjustment to gross income, of limited amount of foreign housing expense paid by a self-employed taxpayer. The deduction is for income tax purposes only and does not reduce self-employment tax.

Resident aliens must meet only the physical presence test - present in the specific country 330 full days during 12 consecutive months. It's complicated!

However, all this may be worth it if you love working in a foreign country, and you are happy with your working and living arrangements.

Social Security

The best time to start collecting Social Security benefits depends on a number of factors:

> Whether or not the taxpayer will have any benefits taken back for earning too much income prior to full retirement age.
>
> The rate at which Social Security benefits are subject to tax before and after full retirement age.
>
> Whether the taxpayer will lose employer-provided health insurance benefits if the taxpayer retires before the age he or she qualifies for Medicare.
>
> Whether the taxpayer's spouse will also have his or her Social Security benefits permanently reduced if the taxpayer retires early.

The taxpayer should review his or her Social Security benefits statement each year to compare the amount of projected benefits linked to the age when they start collecting. Using the above factors, make a comparison calculation and project the income against the tax, as well as, the benefits to determine at which age you should begin collecting Social Security benefits. The Social Security benefits statement can be accessed at www.socialsecurity.gov/?mystatement.

Stay at Home vs Working

The decision to stay at home with a young child versus going to work and paying for day care costs sometimes depends on tax credits that are available to parents with children. You may have a well-paying job, and paying for day care is worth it. A taxpayer with a lower paying job and a spouse who earns enough to support the family may feel the cost of day care is not worth the extra effort. A single taxpayer with a child may find that tax incentives for working parents are either too good to pass up, or barely beneficial, so staying home is the reasonable option.

Aside from taxes, what are the other benefits and costs to working outside the home?

Consider the difference in the quality of a child's day with other adults and children versus spending that time with a parent.

Consider the self-worth of a parent giving up a professional career and potential company advancements to stay at home with his or her child.

Consider the need for an adult to interact with other co-workers versus staying at home and being around children all day with little or no adult companionship. The day care/work question should include asking about the quality of life for the parent as well as the child.

New Tax Laws and Changes Planning

Every year we have changes in our tax laws, and everyone should make sure they check this out. As you have seen, the language is complicated, the requirements can be difficult to figure out. Tax credits expire, and laws are extended or eliminated. It's all in that new 73,954-page manual. Don't file without it.

13.

Retirement, A New Chapter

What does retirement mean? What does it look like? What does it feel like? Why do I want to? How do I want to retire? Where do I want to retire?

What does this mean to me? You may be too young to consider retirement, even after everything we've discussed.

But for those nearing retirement age, consider some of these questions before the year you leave your fulltime employment. Are you going to stop working? Will you change careers instead? Is this your opportunity to start your own business or to pursue the hobbies you could never indulge in while working fulltime. Will you still be supporting your family?

Am I going to stop working, work part time, change careers by starting my own business, or start a hobby that I was never able to before since I needed to provide for family?

History of Retirement and Old Age

Until the late 19th century, how to fill your time wasn't much of a problem. In the new industrial age, a person worked until they died, either from illness or the work itself.

In 1889 German Chancellor Otto von Bismarck offered pensions for the first time. He wasn't necessarily being kind, rather he was hoping to get ahead of a grown Socialist movement (sound familiar?). As self-serving as this benefit was, the idea grew and crossed borders.

In 1875, American Express offered America's first employer-provided retirement plan. Five years later, the Baltimore and Ohio Railroad introduced their first retirement plan, financed jointly by contributions from an employer and its workers.

Once private industry got on board, about a hundred years after Thomas Paine, private pension plans grew.

During World War II, companies needed workers so badly they offered pensions and benefits to attract workers.

During the Depression, the US Government created what we know as Social Security, the idea that the elderly should not live in poverty. In the 1980s many countries lowered the age that a person could collect their pension and Social Security in order to make room for a younger generation of workers. Now countries are facing the opposite challenge: funding a growing elderly population.

Now governments are reversing those policies and raising retirement ages to prevent aging populations from breaking government budgets. Along with that, older people now enjoy better health and are able to work longer. As of 2015, 18.6% of Americans 65 and older were working or looking for work. That was up from a record-low of 10.4% in January 1985, according to Labor Department figures dated 1948.

The idea of providing financial security for the aged gradually expanded throughout Europe and the United States. Bismarck couldn't have imagined retirement lasting two or three decades. Because life expectancy has increased, countries with retirement plans, like social security, are struggling with government pension plans they can no longer afford.

The pension Bismarck offered was the first to be widely

available, but it was not the world's first. In 13 BC, the Roman Emperor Augustus began paying pensions to Roman Legionnaires who had served 20 years in the army. The troops' pensions were financed at first by regular taxes, then by a 5% inheritance tax, (according Frank Eich in *Capturing the British and German Zeitgeist: Impressions and Lessons from the First Years of the New Century*).

In the 16th century, Britain and several European countries offered pensions to their troops, starting with officers and gradually expanding to enlisted men. The first civilian public servant known to have received a pension was an official with the London port authority. In 1684, he was paid half his working income - deducted from the pay of his replacement.

Thomas Paine, the Revolutionary War firebrand famous for his essay *Common Sense*, called for a 10% inheritance tax. Part of the tax was to be used to pay benefits to everyone age 50 and older to "guard against poverty in old age," according to a history by the Social Security Administration.

The idea went nowhere.

After the Civil War, the U.S. government paid pensions to disabled or impoverished Union veterans or to the widows of the dead. Southern states paid pensions to disabled Confederate veterans. The Civil War pensions became a basis for Social Security decades later.

When farming dominated the economy, most men worked as long as their health held out. As they aged, though, they often cut their hours and turned the most physically demanding chores over to sons or hired hands. In 1880, when half of Americans worked on a farm, 78% percent of American men worked past age 65.

As factories began to replace farms in economic importance, skeptics wondered whether old folks could understand and work with the new machines. One of the giants of American medicine, Johns Hopkins Hospital co-founder William Osler, in 1905 announced the “uselessness” of men older than 60 and said the good news is that in general, they should leave the workforce.

Growing prosperity means more people can afford to stop working late in life.

In 1875, American Express offered America’s first employer-provided retirement plan. Five years later, the Baltimore and Ohio Railroad introduced their first retirement plan, financed jointly by contributions from an employer and its workers.

From there, private pension plans grew. In the United States, the plans received a boost during World War II, when the government imposed wage freezes. That led some companies to offer pensions and other benefits to attract workers.

The United States created Social Security in 1935 and added Medicare health benefits for the elderly in 1965. In the 1980s, many countries lowered the age at which people could retire and collect full benefits. This step was part of an effort to clear older workers out of the labor force to make way for the young.

Now, governments are reversing those policies and raising retirement ages to prevent aging populations from breaking government budgets. Along with that, older people now enjoy better health and are able to work longer. As of 2015, 18.6% percent of Americans 65 and older were working or looking for work. That was up from a record-low of 10.4% percent in January 1985, according to Labor Department figures dating to 1948.

Retirement is considered is the point where a person stops employment completely. A person may also semi-retire by reducing work hours.

An increasing number of individuals are choosing to put off total retirement by starting a new career or by working part-time, not necessarily because they have to but because they love what they do.

Many people choose to retire when they are eligible for private or public pension benefits, although some are forced to retire when physical conditions no longer allow them to work any longer (usually by illness or accident) or as a result of legislation concerning their position.

Nowadays most developed countries have systems to provide pensions in old age, which may be sponsored by employers and/or the state. In many poorer countries, support for the old is still mainly provided through the family. Today retirement with a pension is considered a right of the worker in many societies and an entitlement from the U.S. government.

The "standard" retirement age varies from country to country, but it is generally between the ages of 50 to 70. In some countries, the age range is different for males and females, although this has recently been challenged in some countries (e.g. Austria), and in some countries the ages are being changed to reflect the times.

In France, the retirement age will be increased from age 62 to age 67 over the next eight years. Spain's retirement age will be extended from 63 to 67 by 2027.

In the United States, while the normal retirement age for Social Security, or Old Age Survivors Insurance (OASI), historically has been age 65 to receive unreduced benefits, it is gradually increasing to age 67. For those turning 65 in 2008, full benefits will be payable beginning at age 66.

Public servants are often not covered by Social Security but have their own pension programs. Police officers in the United States are typically allowed to retire at half pay after only 20 years of service or three-quarter pay after 30 years, allowing people to retire in their early forties or fifties. Military members of the US Armed Forces may elect to retire after 20 years of active duty. Their retirement pays (not a pension since they can be involuntarily called back to active duty at any time) is calculated on total number of years on active duty, their final pay grade and the retirement system in place when they entered service.

Allowances such as housing and subsistence are not used to calculate a member's retired pay. Members awarded the Medal of Honor qualify for a separate stipend, regardless of the years of service. Military members in the reserve and US National Guard have their retirement based on a point system.

From *Wikipedia*, (https://en.wikipedia.org/wiki/Retirement) see also http://www.investopedia.com.

How do you know how much money you'll need for retirement? One way to check it out is to use the Monte Carlo simulation. The Monte Carlo simulation supplies a range of possible outcomes for any action. The software will help you gain understanding of the amounts you'll need and the steps in your retirement journey. The simulation results show the probability of how successful your chosen retirement plan will be.

Anyone can retire at any time. But generally, people

don't qualify for support from their governments before a certain set age. Thus, to retire early you'll need to rely on your own savings and investments to self-support. This may include a buy out from your company, saved money, or investments.

Savings Needed for Early Retirement

Those contemplating early retirement will want to know if they have enough to survive a potential bear market. If your stocks and bonds do not grow at the same rate as today, what will you do?

The 4% rule withdrawing 4% of your savings as income - is no longer considered a rule of thumb. We now look at the whole picture and the needs of the client. Time, rate of return, risk, and the needs of the client are critical.

When retiring prior to age $59^{1/2}$, there is a 10% IRS penalty on withdrawals from a retirement plan such as a 401(k) plan or a Traditional IRA. Exceptions apply under certain circumstances. After this age, the penalty-free status is achieved, and the 10% IRS penalty no longer applies.

To avoid the 10% penalty prior to age $59^{1/2}$, a person should consult a tax professional about the use of IRS rule 72 T. It allows the distribution of an IRA account prior to age $59^{1/2}$ in equal amounts of a period of either 5 years or until the age of $59^{1/2}$ (whichever is the longest time period), without a 10% penalty. Taxes still must be paid on the distributions.

The effects of making inflation-adjusted withdrawals from a given starting portfolio can be modeled with special software that uses historical stock market data to estimate likely portfolio returns. Another approach is to employ a retirement calculator that also uses historical stock market modeling, but it adds provisions for incorporating pensions other retirement income and changes in spending that may occur during the course of the retirement.

Life After Retirement

Retirement might coincide with important life changes; a retired worker might move to a new location (e.g. a retirement community). Living in a new location may mean reduced contact with their previous social circle as well as adopting a new lifestyle. Often retirees volunteer for charities and other community organizations. Traveling is a common retirement goal, and for some it becomes a way of life, often called so-called grey nomads. Some retired people choose to go and live in warmer climates, in what is known as "retirement migration".

It has been found that Americans have five lifestyle choices as they age:

Work full-time .

Work part-time.

Retire from work and become engaged in a variety of leisure and recreational activities.

Retire from work & later return to work part-time.

Retire from work & later return to work full-time.

An important note to make is that four of the five choices involve working. America is facing an important demographic change as the Baby Boomer generation reaches retirement age. This poses two questions: whether there will be a sufficient number of skilled workers in the work force, and whether the current pension programs will be sufficient to support the growing number of retired people.

The reasons that some people choose to never retire, or to return to work after retiring include not only the difficulty of planning for retirement but also the desire to earn wages and fringe benefits, to expend physical and mental energy, to produce goods and services, to experience social interaction, and social status.

Often retirees are called upon to care for grandchildren and occasionally aged parents. For many, retirement gives them more time to devote to a hobby or sports, such as golf or sailing. On the other hand, many retirees feel restless and suffer from depression as a result of their new situation. Although it is not scientifically possible to directly show that retirement either causes or contributes to depression, the newly retired are one of the most vulnerable social groups. Sometimes retirement coincides with deterioration of one's health and it is believed this plays a major role in increased rates of depression in retirees.

When studies have been made about the healthy elderly and retired, people found to be as happy or happier as younger employed adults; therefore, retirement in and of itself is not likely to contribute to development of depression. It is far more likely that the lack of health is the biggest contributor.

Many people in the later years of their lives, due to failing health, require assistance, sometimes in the form of expensive treatments provided nursing homes. Those who need care, but are not in need of constant assistance, may choose to live in a retirement home, assisted living, or retirement community.

14.

Estate & Legacy

Beneficiaries – Who Gets What

Whenever you hear that an estate "went into probate" (which means that the courts handle and distribute your estate), the audience sucks in their breath in a collective gasp. Probate, it would seem, is a dirty word, one you do not want to say out loud.

What can you do? Do you want a big piece of your hard - earned income to siphon directly to the government? Or do you want more control?

If you want more control, consider these top ten mistakes listed at the *American Association of*

Individual Investors (AAII.com).

Top 10 Mistakes with Beneficiaries and Probate

1. Not Naming a Beneficiary

Not naming a beneficiary on your life insurance policy or retirement account, will likely guaranteed that the asset will go through probate upon your death. Further, for a retirement account, this could create some avoidable tax consequences. The company holding your asset may have contract provisions designating default beneficiaries that could be completely inconsistent with your estate planning goals. Even if your estate is your beneficiary, you should complete a beneficiary designation form.

2. Not Designating Contingent Beneficiaries

Often, an account holder will designate a primary beneficiary when an account is initially established but will fail to designate any contingent beneficiaries. If your primary beneficiary (your spouse, for example) predeceases you, or if you die together or before you have had an opportunity to designate a new beneficiary, then the same consequences will result as if you had not named a beneficiary at all.

3. Failing to Keep Beneficiary Designations Up-to-Date

First and foremost, if you get divorced, it is *essential*

that you immediately review and update all beneficiary designations! If your ex-spouse is still named as your beneficiary upon your death, then the company holding your asset will most likely distribute the asset directly to your ex-spouse even if you are remarried to someone else.

I had a client who suffered through a very bad divorce. Ten years later he still harbored bad feelings about his ex-wife. Yet every time we reviewed his finances, he put off changing his insurance beneficiary. The last time we reviewed this issue was 2014. Two days after that review, he suffered a heart attack and died. You guessed it, his life insurance went to his ex-wife. All along he wanted his daughters to share his insurance, but because he did not make the official change, it didn't happen. I see this all the time. Many of us end up giving wealth to the wrong people simply because we are unwilling to take 10 minutes to make the changes.

Further, if your primary beneficiary predeceases you, then it is essential to review and update your beneficiary designations at that time to ensure your beneficiaries remain consistent with your estate planning goals. In other words, make sure the people to whom you leave your money are still alive to enjoy it.

4. Naming Minors as Direct Beneficiaries

Many parents establish testamentary trusts within their wills. They designate a specific age at which their children may have control over their assets. In the meantime, a trustee (who may or may not be the same person named as the child's guardian) is named as the manager of those assets until the child has reached the designated age. Most often, the assets are available in the at the trustee's discretion for the child's health, education, maintenance or support.

However, regardless of the provisions contained in your will, if you name a minor child as the direct beneficiary of your life insurance policy, the proceeds will most likely be paid out to your child outright as soon as he or she reaches the age of 18. Considering that the average inheritance is spent in about 18 months, providing an 18-year-old with immediate access to a large sum of money is probably not in his or her best interest.

Generally, if you have minor children and no living trust, it is better to name your estate as your beneficiary and allow the proceeds to go through the probate process in order to ensure they are distributed to the testamentary trusts established for your children according to the terms of your will.

5. Naming Special Needs Individuals as Direct Beneficiaries

If you name a "special needs" individual (i.e., a person who is receiving a governmental benefit such as Supplemental Security Income (SSI) or medical assistance based on a disability) as a direct beneficiary, you could unintentionally disqualify that individual from receiving his or her valuable governmental benefits. The individual must then "spend down" the inheritance and, after virtually all the money has been spent, go through the application process again. This "spend down" effectively defeats the purpose of naming a beneficiary!

If you wish to leave an inheritance for a loved one who is receiving this type of assistance, it is much better to create a "special needs trust," also known as a "supplemental needs trust," within your will or living trust to hold the inheritance for the benefit of that individual for his or her lifetime without jeopardizing his or her benefits.

6. Naming Financially Irresponsible Beneficiaries

Many of us have loved ones who have repeatedly demonstrated that they will never be financially responsible. Clearly, naming this type of individual as a direct beneficiary may serve only to contribute to a gambling or drug addiction, or result in assets being claimed by creditors in a bankruptcy or income tax proceeding.

Often, it is better to create a lifetime "spendthrift trust" to hold the inheritance for the benefit of that individual for his or her lifetime while protecting the assets from creditors.

Jane and Paul came to my office to do Financial & legacy planning, they are in their 80's and have no one left to leave their estate to but their son Michael who is 43. Michael is irresponsible and they feel unable to take care of the assets that they would leave him. Sadly, their only child has been arrested for drug use and is currently on probation. They are providing Michael with a house they own, and set him up with a job helping his dad maintain real estate rental properties they own.

They are reasonably concerned that Michael would not manage a direct inheritance. Michael's parents worked hard to amass over ten million in assets, and they don't want to see it all quickly disappear. What should they do? This is becoming increasingly the norm for many parents. Helping parents make good decisions is my job.

7. Naming Direct Beneficiaries on All Assets Other than Real Estate

If you own real estate titled solely in your name (or titled as a tenant in common) upon your death, the real estate interest will need to go through the probate process before it can pass to your beneficiaries, even if you have a will in place.

It is not unusual for the death probate process to take a year or longer. In the meantime, before your real estate can be sold or distributed, your estate is responsible for paying maintenance expenses including, but not limited to, real estate taxes, insurance, utilities, maintenance and general upkeep of the property. Your estate is also responsible for your final debts and expenses, including your funeral bill, court costs and attorney's fees.

If you have insufficient cash available within your estate, then your children or other beneficiaries will need to find a way to pay these costs. However, they are under no legal obligation to pay these costs from life insurance proceeds, cash received through POD designations, etc.

Therefore, if you own real estate that will go through probate upon your death, it is generally advisable to also allow your cash accounts and/or life insurance proceeds to go through probate as well in order to eliminate situations such as the one described above.

8. Naming Multiple Beneficiaries on a Transfer on Death Deed

Some states allow a special type of deed known as "transfer on death deed" or "Lady Bird deed." Through this type of deed, you can designate a beneficiary or beneficiaries who will inherit your real estate outside of probate upon your death.

If you have only one child who is a responsible adult, and who is not a special needs individual, then this strategy may work well. However, if you have multiple beneficiaries, then a transfer on death deed is most likely not a good option. If multiple individuals own a single piece of real estate, they all must agree on the Realtor and the sale price, and until the property is sold all owners should contribute equally to the maintenance of the property needing cash to make sure the property is well kept for all users.

For obvious reasons, this arrangement can create more trouble and family disputes than might have occurred had the property gone through an organized probate proceeding and remained in the control of a single designated personal representative.

9. Naming a Child as a Co-Owner of a Deposit or Investment Account

In his or her later years, a parent will sometimes add a trusted adult child as the co-owner of his or her bank account(s). The purpose of this arrangement is usually to allow the child to assist the parent in managing his or her finances, signing checks, etc. Generally, the intent is not for this child to inherit the entire balance of the account upon the parent's death to the exclusion of the other children.

There are numerous potential issues with this arrangement, some of which are outlined below.

Gifting: When you add your child (or anyone else) as the co-owner of your asset, you have just legally gifted them half the value of the asset. Currently, you can gift up to $14,000 per year per beneficiary without incurring any gift tax consequences. If the value you have "gifted" is greater than this amount, then you are legally required to file a gift tax return and incur any gift tax consequences associated with the transfer.

Creditor Issues: Once your child (or anyone else) becomes the co-owner of your account, half of your account will then become subject to the claims of that person's creditors. Therefore, if the co-owner gets sued or files for bankruptcy, then half of your account could end up in the hands of his or her creditors. Your account could even become an issue as part of your child's divorce proceeding!

Final Expenses: Even if your intent is for the money in your account to be used to pay your funeral expenses after your death, the child you have named as a co-owner of your account is under no legal obligation to use this money for its intended purpose. He or she could simply walk away with the account balance, leaving the other assets in your estate to pay for these expenses, resulting in a "windfall" for that child.

By employing other estate planning techniques, you can better accomplish your estate planning objectives without putting your account at risk. For example, you can create a durable power of attorney naming your trusted child as the agent to manage your account during your lifetime. You can then either add a POD designation to the account, or allow the account to go through probate upon your death with the rest of your probate estate. As a final alternative, you could create a living trust and title the account in the name of your living trust.

10. Naming One Child as the Sole Beneficiary of a Life Insurance Policy or Deposit Account

A parent with multiple adult children will sometimes designate one child as the sole beneficiary of a life insurance policy or deposit account, with the intent that this child will use the proceeds to pay for funeral and other final expenses and then distribute the remaining balance equally among his or her siblings.

Similar to the co-owner situation referenced above, the child you have named as your beneficiary is under no legal obligation to use this money for its intended purpose and could simply walk away with the account balance. Further, your child may be unable to distribute the account balance to his or her siblings without incurring his or her own gift tax consequences.

Why plan at all? Will it matter? Yes. Your children and grandchild depend on you to make the right decisions. Even more important, plan while you are young, would you want to leave your spouse or young children at the mercy of the courts? Or do you want to make sure they are well taken care of. How you handle your estate is the final gesture and demonstration of your love.

On that note, re-visit your life insurance every two years regardless if any changes in your life. Changes include divorce, moving to another state, children who are no longer minors (does your thirty-year-old really want Aunt Susie as a guardian?) changing jobs, and planning to retire to cover some lifestyle changes. I understand that it is an agonizing situation to review these documents; however, the more you review them the more you will understand what you are trying to achieve.

By working to educate yourself, you will provide your family with the best protection possible, and you will not wonder whether costs will be covered by the assets you leave to your heirs. Overall it will make you feel better.

The Bonus Mistake: IRA Beneficiary Trust

One bonus mistake people make is creating an IRA beneficiary trust. Sometimes this may be a good option. This trust is designed to be named as the beneficiary of an IRA, and upon the death of the IRA owner, to hold the IRA assets in trust for the protection and benefit of another family member.

However, this type of trust may create unnecessary complexities rather than easing the post-death administration process for your loved ones. Ask: "Is there a strong reason to name a trust as the IRA beneficiary or is there a way to achieve planning goals without the risks and complexities of naming a trust?" This is a big trap and can have very bad consequences.

John, Mollie, Edward & Patrick came to see me after they realized that their parent's trust had been named as IRA beneficiary. What could they do about this? Their parent's full one million dollars of retirement money had to be cashed out with taxes paid on distribution.

What their parent did not understand, by not naming an individual as the beneficiary, they lost the opportunity to use a five-year or a stretch IRA, which would allow them to not pay taxes now, but be able to pay over time. Now they had no option but to pay a lump sum to the IRS. This may have been good for the estate if the only cash was the retirement account, if they had real estate to maintain, and if there were no other taxes to pay, but they did not, and the windfall ended up being a burden.

Joint Tenancy

If you put an asset in joint tenancy, then upon your death, title to that asset will pass outside of probate to the surviving owner(s). The advantage of this is to avoid probate and make a direct beneficiary distribution.

However, the limitation of this designation is to that asset only. Some disadvantages include inadvertent gifting of the joint tenant interest, possible guardianship for minors, misuse by irresponsible beneficiaries, loss of benefits to special needs beneficiaries, exposure to creditors of the other joint tenant(s), and loss to the estate of needed funds. The asset is still susceptible to adult guardianship jurisdiction if you become incompetent, and this is another form of probate (sometimes called “living probate”).

Important note regarding cost basis: When you gift an asset to a beneficiary during your lifetime (i.e., naming a beneficiary as a joint tenant or co-owner), the beneficiary inherits your original cost basis as to the interest gifted. Conversely, were your beneficiary to inherit the asset *upon your death*, the entire asset would receive a “step-up” in cost basis on your date of death, resulting in a possible reduction or elimination of the capital gains tax upon subsequent sale of the asset.

Please make sure you understand when implementing joint tenancy as a gifting or probate avoidance strategy with a large or highly appreciated asset unless you have first consulted with an estate planning attorney and an EA or CPA.

Payable on Death (POD)

If you have designated a “POD” beneficiary on your bank account, then the account will be paid on your death directly to the named beneficiary(ies). As with joint tenancy, the advantage of POD is to avoid probate and make a direct beneficiary distribution as to that particular asset.

Again, the designation is limited to that asset only. Other disadvantages include possible guardianship for minors, misuse by irresponsible beneficiaries, loss of benefits to special needs beneficiaries, and loss to the estate of needed funds.

Note, the asset is still susceptible to living probate if you become incompetent.

Transfer on Death (TOD)

If you have designated a "TOD" beneficiary on your investment account or real estate property, then that asset will be transferred on your death directly to the named beneficiary(ies).

If an account is involved, then the same advantages and disadvantages apply to TOD as to the POD designations described in the preceding paragraph. The asset is susceptible to living probate.

When a TOD designation is placed against real estate, additional disadvantages are presented: First, if you have a lone beneficiary, he or she could die before you eliminate a non-probate beneficiary, redirecting your estate back to a distant heir or resulting in a death probate. Second, if you have multiple beneficiaries, you have created problems inherent in leaderless group action.

Beneficiary Designations

If you have named a direct beneficiary on your life insurance policy or retirement account, then that asset will pass directly to the named beneficiary(ies) on your death.

Here, the same advantages and disadvantages apply as to the non–real estate TOD and POD designations discussed previously. The asset is susceptible to living probate and to many mistakes. I have also found that people consistently forgetting to name beneficiaries on insurance or retirement accounts, fail to designate a contingent beneficiary, and fail to update after marriage, divorce, birth or death.

Additionally, people often seem perfectly willing to have huge sums of insurance proceeds or retirement funds distributed to their beneficiaries without any structural protections or attention to alternative tax-deferral mechanisms. They simply write a name on a form. This will not achieve protection against predators, creditors or potential ex-spouses of the beneficiary. Also, it will not preserve an inherited IRA from seizure in bankruptcy court nor encourage the beneficiary to maintain tax-deferral on the retirement account.

Living Trust

Any asset titled in the name of your living trust will not go through probate. The only documentation your successor trustee will need at the time of your death will be your death certificate and your certificate of trust. The asset will ultimately pass to your beneficiaries privately and according to the terms of your living trust. Moreover, living probate (adult guardianship) over your assets is avoided.

In the trust, this well provide structural protections for you and beneficiaries in relation to the designations you have made on insurance, retirement, brokerage or deposit accounts, and even with respect to real estate. The trust can also provide alternative tax-deferral mechanisms on qualified accounts. This level of planning is not available by merely completing a simple beneficiary designation form alone.

The primary disadvantage of a living trust is that the legal fees involved with creating a comprehensive living trust - based estate plan are more expensive than those involved with creating a will-based estate plan. In most situations, this cost is far less than the legal fees and other costs associated with a potential death probate or living probate. If you desire court involvement and oversight with regard to the management and distribution of your assets upon your death or incompetency, then a living trust may not be suitable for you.

At what age do you need to worry about your estate? There is no set age, but if I was to start thinking about it, I would say it was the age of majority (the age when a person is legally considered a full adult in most cultures: 18 to 21). If you are mature and can legally drink, then you need to worry about the unimaginable future - it's part of the package. The first thing to consider, as we mentioned before, is who will take care of your affairs if you can't. At the very least, name your executer or trustee. They will be able to take care of your assets in your name.

What is an estate and why do I need to do anything about it?

An estate starts when you have a job with salary, and you have not yet collected your accumulated paycheck, vacation pay, retirement, stocks and options, and other assets that are with your employer. Your executer or power of attorney (if you are alive) can make arrangements to cash your checks and to use them for your care and your bills. The executer can sell your car should you need money for your care. If you live in an apartment, you have belongings that may need to be moved. Someone should have access to your social media accounts. You can see where this is going. A will, trust, health directive, living will and power of attorney names the person who legally has the right to take care of your assets, legal affairs, and personal body health decisions (which also includes funeral arrangements). In other words, name the person who can legally touch your stuff.

When you have not communicated what you want by making an estate plan you become open to abuse. You risk having your assets stolen or awarded to someone you may hate or distrust. The law is not fair; it is the law.

Remember the famous comedian and actor Groucho Marx? He did not have the proper documents to protect himself and his estate. His nieces and nephews decided they could make better decisions then he could. They took him to court and were able to take over. He lost control of his assets and his life. If the right documents had been in place, Groucho would have had the people he wanted to help him make the right decisions.

Be sure to revisit your documents every two years as they may become invalid due to changes in the law. You also may have forgotten what you wrote in your documents. Examples of famous people that ended up with invalid wills are Abraham Lincoln, Ulysses S. Grant, Martin Luther King, and Buddy Holly. Granted they were busy. Famous people with valid wills include Marilyn Monroe, Elvis Presley, Jacklyn Kennedy Onassis, and Paul Newman.

Of course, this is not just about you. It's also about your

family members. Do they have their wishes in writing? Are you sure their wills are up to date? A conversation with your parents or children about arrangements is extremely important, but often difficult. No one wants to talk about death. But it is critical.

A place to start is to listen to your parents or grandparents. What is their story? Even if you think you've heard this one before, listen again with the intent to uncover their real fears and values. Do they value money? Do they want to leave a legacy? Are they worried about their end of life comfort and dignity?

Plan accordingly with those goals and values in mind.

Conversely, if you are the parent or grandparent in question, make your values known to your family. What do you want?

Are your parents frugal and feel it is too expensive to pay for the legal advice to amend the will or trust? Explain to them that their current documentation may not be valid because of the changes in the law. The cost later will be far greater than the cost right now to update their will.

Review and make sure their will is updated every two years.

Trusts

Trusts are valuable estate planning devices that allow

for the transmission of wealth with lower tax liability. With proper estate management, a trust will also create income, potentially allowing for the trust to last in perpetuity. Trusts also allow for the beneficiaries to pull income from the corpus (body) of the trust, yet insure that their creditors cannot obtain the income producing assets themselves.

The same fail-safe plan also applies for a financially irresponsible beneficiary (I know, you're looking at your brother), in that it provides income but prevents the financially irresponsible beneficiary from squandering the income producing asset.

One of the most popular types of trusts is the irrevocable trust. As with anything in life, there are upsides and downsides; one of the downsides is that in most circumstances, and, more particularly most states, an irrevocable trust is just that - water tight. Unwinding an irrevocable trust when it no longer functions as it should be possible but must be done correctly. The good news is that assets from the trust may be transferred or gifted to the beneficiaries or the settlor (if still alive).

There are times when a trust no longer accomplishes the stated intention of the settlor. For example, in December 2010 Congress raised the estate tax exemption to five million dollars, but for only two years. So, at the end of 2012 many people thought that the estate and gift tax exemption was going to go back down to the previous one million dollars. To counter this, they created irrevocable trusts.

We now know that Congress made that heightened estate and gift tax exemptions permanent. In addition, in 2011, Congress allowed for a surviving spouse to inherit any unused estate tax exemption, making it portable. In the past, individuals created trusts that would optimize a lower tax amount, believing that the much lower estate and gift tax exemptions would remain.

Additionally, let us not forget that personality conflict occurs. Sometimes there may be very valid professional reasons why a beneficiary may want to do things according to instructions and values of the settlor. The trustee may have other values and ways of doing things that are contrary to the original intent of the creator of the trust.

Changing an irrevocable trust requires really good reasons, like changes in the law. You absolutely need a good attorney for this one. Make sure he or she is experienced in Wills and Trust, and knows the applicable state laws.

Wealth and Children

If you are a parent who worries about what your wealth will do to your children, you are not alone. Many clients want to leave money to their kids, but they are concerned that their children are unable to handle sudden wealth. Some worry that providing too much money to their children will rob them of ambition and hard work. Others don't want to squander the wealth it took them so long to accumulate.

CNN news host Anderson Cooper is the son of Gloria Vanderbilt - a successful fashion and interior designer and daughter to the Vanderbilt railroad and shipping empire. She is said to be worth $200 million. In an interview with Howard Stern, Anderson commented: "I don't believe in inheriting money. I think it's an initiative sucker. I think it's a curse." Cooper continued, "who has inherited a lot of money that has gone on to do things in their own life?" When Stern reminded him that his mother did this, Anderson responded, "I think that's an anomaly."

What is your view on inherited money? Is it an "initiative sucker," or can it be used to create a better and more fulfilled life? I believe that sudden wealth can be positive and contribute to a fulfilled life. Yes, it can cause some to lose their drive and ambition, but with the proper work and structure, those who inherit can use the money as a tool to create meaningful lives of their own. But still, many parents are not convinced. They are not hoping their children will be visited by a sudden flash of financial judgment. They are taking action to make sure they provide for, not tempt, their children with an influx of sudden wealth.

If you are concern about gifting or leaving your children an inheritance, consider the following.

1. Give your kids a financial test.

Each person can gift up to $14,000 (stuck at this level since 2014) per year to as many people as they wish without any gift tax consequence. If you are married, combined you and your spouse can give $28,000 per person. Some parents gift their children money without any restrictions or rules, and then sit back and watch what happens. How will your children handle a $5+ million inheritance? Why don't you see what they do with $20,000 first? Do they save it? Do they ask for help? Do they pay off debt? Do they blow it in Vegas?

2. Use incentive trusts.

The fear of many parents (and apparently, Anderson Cooper) is that too much money can squash ambition and drive. One of the fears that keeps many affluent parents up at night is the idea that their kids will be robbed of the motivation and spirit they need to make an impact.

The solution is to create an incentive trust. This kind of trust spells out what a child needs to do and then matches their efforts. One of the common incentives trusts is an "investment banker clause." This trust matches the child's income. If Jane makes $75,000 from her job, the trust will distribute $75,000 each year. If her younger brother Bill spends too much time playing and only makes $22,000 a year, the trust will distribute just $22,000 to him.

You can also put a base amount on this incentive; a child must earn a minimum (e.g. $20,000 or $30,000 per year) to receive a match. This kind of incentive allows your heirs to become strong and self-efficient, and it rewards effort.

But what if Jane wants to join the Peace Corps? You can add language that will ensure distributions if your child is involved in a non-profit. Again, the sky is the limit when it comes to drafting who gets what and when. Newport Beach estate planning attorney Cheryl Barrett says, "I often build educational incentives in parents' and grandparents' trusts that are designed to reward the beneficiaries' educational accomplishments."

For example, the trustee might be directed to disburse $10,000 upon attainment of a Bachelor's degree and $20,000 upon attainment of a Master's or Doctorate degree. While Barrett acknowledges that a degree is not a guarantee of a beneficiary's personal success, she states, "The pursuit of it requires vision, goal setting, and engagement with other motivated individuals, all of which enhance a beneficiary's likelihood of success."

3. Distribute money based on age and events.

Do you think 20-year-old you would have been ready for large wealth? Yeah, me neither. Parents can design their trust so that their kids get a small amount of money each year and larger amounts when they reach certain ages (30, 35, and 40). They can also allow for trust distributions to pay for college expenses, weddings, or house down payments. A popular strategy is to distribute income from the trust assets when the kids are young and then to distribute principal when they are older and, ideally, have a career and greater financial sophistication.

4. Get your kids involved in a personal foundation.

If you have children still living with you, creating a personal foundation can be a wonderful opportunity to support causes you believe in, get a nice tax deduction, and more importantly to our point, to teach kids about money. Create a personal foundation and require that 5% of the foundation's balance must be distributed each year. You can assign family members the responsibility of researching a cause and donating say, 1%. This gives the kids a chance to impact their world and to make good choices. Make it fun and joyful.

5. Gifting without giving cash directly to your children.

With the $14,000 exemption, you can directly pay down student loans and mortgages. The difference this will make in your child's future will be significant, and you will not be putting cash in their hands. Make sure there are no prepayment penalties on mortgage loans. It is a fact that mortgages and school loans have a significant role in today's world and reducing that debt load will make a big difference in your children's lives.

As a parent, you want what is best for your kids. It's natural to worry how a large inheritance will affect their drive and choices for life. With some planning, money can be a tool that enriches their lives rather than an anchor that drags them down. Consider the strategies above and talk to your certified financial planner and estate attorney for more ideas.

Affluent Americans are committed to building a legacy both by using their wealth in positive ways and by passing their values on to future generations. Be part of the solution and part of creating a better future.

15.

Who to Work With - Finding the Right Professional

You may think by reading my book you now know everything about finances and do not need any professional help. However, your finances and financial future is not a DIY project. There is no quick fix. This is not only your life, but the lives of many people, all of whom you probably dearly love.

This book is about giving overall looks at your potential options. However, there is no way this small book can cover and fully explain every available option, as everyone is different and in their own unique situation.

This chapter will provide you with information about different types of financial advisors and professionals who can help you make good decisions. I recommend the use of a Certified Financial Planner. There are different ways to find a good CFP®, and I will give you some recommendations to help you make the right decisions about your wealth and how to best manage it.

Certified Financial Planner (CFP®)

A CFP® must adhere to the CFP® Board's code of ethics and any additional mandates. They provide financial planning services as a fiduciary, meaning they act for their client's best interest.

CFP®s must complete a comprehensive course of study that covers the six disciplines of financial planning: Financial Planning, Investments, Insurance & Risk, Retirement Planning, Tax Planning, and Estate Planning. They must additionally, have a bachelor's degree from a regional accredited college or university.

The CFP® professional must pass a CFP® Board comprehensive examination that covers six disciplines; Financial Planning, Investments, Insurance & risk, Retirement Planning, Tax Planning, and Estate Planning, which tests an individual's ability to integrate and apply their financial planning knowledge.

They can help you with:

Setting realistic financial and personal goals

The CFP® will work with you to assess your current financial health by analyzing your assets, debts, income, insurance, taxes, investments, and estate & legacy plans.

Putting a plan in action and monitoring the progress

A good CFP® continues to work with you so that you stay focused with your vision setting priorities and meeting your life goals. He or she will also keep you informed of the changes in the tax law.

Other good reasons to hire at CFP®:

Retirement - making sure the money will last.

Handling an inheritance or a large sum of money or instant wealth, beyond what you are used to handling.

Preparing for marriage or divorce.

Planning for the birth or adoption of a child.

Facing a serious illness, layoff, or natural disaster.

Caring for aging parents or disabled child .

Coping financially with the death of a spouse,

family member, or friend .

Planning for college or education.

Dealing with complex financial issues such as the calculation of social security and tax strategies to best maximize your income and wealth.

Choosing a Certified Financial Planner is as important as choosing a doctor or lawyer. A CFP® is a very personal relationship. Go to cfp.net or plannersearch.org and search by zip code to find those that are close to you.

Most Certified Financial Planners will give you a list to bring to the first or second meeting.

What to bring to your first meeting:

Bank statements.

Pay stubs.

Check registers.

Credit Card balances

Mortgage or loan payments.

List of liabilities (debts).

Completed expense worksheet (past 6 months).

Wills, trusts, healthcare power of attorney, health

care proxy, or other powers of attorney.

Business agreements and contracts.

Titles for homes, cars, real estate, etc.

Retirement account statements.

Social Security statements.

Pension benefit statement and contracts from HR.

Investment statements.

Listing of available investment options in investment and retirement accounts.

Stock Options.

Homeowners and automobile declaration pages for insurances.

Life, disability, or long-term care insurance policies.

Tax returns for the past three years.

Tax estimate for next return (e.g. deductions, credits, etc.).

List of employee benefits.

Fees for Service

Certified Financial planners can be paid in different

ways. Choosing a method, depends on your individual situation. The main thing you should ask is how they charge you and will they make it clear to you how they are compensated or paid.

Commission

Commission is calculated as a percentage of the amount of the sale or purchase. It is transaction based. This may include 12 (b) 1 fees (a mutual fund internal fee for annual marketing, distribution fees and operational expense), trailing commissions, surrender charges, and contingent deferred sales charges.

Fee Only

Fee only comes exclusively from the clients as a fixed, flat, hourly percentage, or as performance-based fees.

Commission and Fee

If the CFP® professional receives or is entitled to receive both commissions and fees for services, they must disclose his or her compensation as "Commission and Fee."

Financial Adviser

A financial advisor is a general category that encompasses many different types of financial professionals. Stockbrokers, insurance agents, tax preparers, investment managers, and financial planners are part of this group. Estate planners and bankers may also be included.

The Investment Advisers Act of 1940 was enacted to regulate the actions of investment Advisers/Advisors.

Advisors are administered by the Securities and Exchange Commission. They usually have a series 6 or 7, (a General Securities Representative Qualification) and are insurance licensed.

Registered Investment Adviser (RIA): An investment adviser registered with the Securities and Exchange Commission or a state's securities agency. They generally manage high-net-worth investors starting at a worth of $1 million or more. This is an individual or firm that receives compensation for giving advice on investing in securities such as stocks, bonds, mutual funds, or exchange traded funds. They are generally paid by percentage of the value of the assets they manage for clients, hourly fee, fixed fee, and a commission on the securities they sell. They must hold the series 65 license.

As you can see there are many different financial professionals you can turn to. I recommend starting with a CFP® and seeing if it's the right fit. Some of us hold not only the CFP® designation, but also the RIA and other licenses.

Attorneys

There are attorneys for every area of law. I am only going to cover a few; if you need more information, do some research on lawyers.com or simply search "What are different types of attorneys?" Then go to types of lawyers and Areas of Law Definitions.

Admiralty and Maritime Lawyers

These lawyers cover business and commercial use of coastal and navigable waters, including lakes, rivers, bays, harbors, and ports.

Adoption Lawyers

Adoption fits under the family law category. It is about establishing parent-child relationships between orphaned children or a child without parents (a child without parents means parent has either relinquished their rights or have abandon the child may have been directed through the courts). This type of lawyer can help people work with adoption agencies, go a non-agency route, access adoption records, and navigate international adoptions.

Breach of Contract Lawyers

Breach of Contract is part of the contract category of law. This is usually when someone fails or refuses to do what they have agreed upon in their contract. Only judge or jury can say whether a breach is material.

Some of the ways a breach can be settled can include injunction, restitution, or money damages.

Business Lawyers This can include business formations like sole proprietorships, partnerships, limited partnerships, limited liability companies, franchises, joint ventures, corporations, and closely held corporations. Attorneys deal with legal issues regarding compliance formation and registration, the requirements for filling for state agencies, drafting the articles of incorporation or partnership agreements, and handling other documents.

Bankruptcy Lawyers

Both debtors (individuals, businesses, or municipalities) who are suddenly unable to pay their debts and creditors alike need a bankruptcy lawyer. The lawyer will help debtors to be freed of their financial debts. A bankruptcy is filed in federal court. There are several types of bankruptcy, and it is important to consult a bankruptcy attorney to help decide what kind of bankruptcy will help your situation.

Divorce Lawyers

The divorce attorney helps you terminate your marriage. They also help determine child custody, child support, spousal support, and the division of marital property, including assets from pensions, retirement plans, savings, and family businesses or assets. They can also help with taxes and determining who and how people will pay for taxes both on the federal and states. They also help with decisions regarding venue, procedures, and the grounds for divorce.

Estate & Legacy Lawyers

This is part of the law is concerned with the legal strategies to help you with accumulated wealth and how to best dispose of it through wills, trusts, charitable bequests, gifts, and other transfers throughout life. Some of the issues an estate lawyer helps with are community property, taxes, nature and validity of wills or trusts, transfers, conveyances, and gifts. The attorney can help define the duties and liabilities of trustees, executors, administrators, or personal representatives; this includes probate practices and procedures. A good lawyer will help protect his or her client's interests from excess taxation during the transfer of wealth.

Immigration Lawyers

Immigration lawyers specialize with the regulation and control of aliens, non-citizens, or immigrants, including admission and removal of aliens or foreigners. They can help with visas, asylum naturalization, immigration crimes, denaturalization, and deportation.

Insurance Lawyers

Insurance law is all about the regulation of the

insurance industry. These specialists help clients with coverage disputes, disclosure requirements, information privacy, handling, and processing, as well as insurance band faith and tort liability.

As you can see, you need to look at what law you are dealing with and search for a qualified attorney that deals with your special circumstance.

Certified Public Accountant (CPA) or Enrolled Agent (EA)

The CPA's are professionals that are only licensed in the states in which they operate. They are also not required to demonstrate their competence in all areas of taxation.

To become a CPA, you must first complete the education requirements of the state you plan to practice in. Once finished, a CPA must sit for the state CPA exam. The CPA exam is a standardized test of 4 different sections: Auditing and Attestation, Business Environment and Concepts, Financial Accounting and Reporting, and Regulation. CPA's are governed by the Department of the Treasury Circular 230.

Some states also require one year of accounting-based work experience under supervision of an active CPA.

The IRS Enrolled Agents' license must meet more stringent requirements. They are the only federally licensed tax experts who specialize in all areas of taxation law and can represent you before the IRS in any state or any U.S. possession. They have received the highest award from the IRS. EA's are known as America's Tax Experts®.

EA's are required to understand not only the complexity of the current tax code and how it affects you, but also to stay current with the constant tax changes.

EA's must pass a stringent testing process to qualify. This includes a background check and finger printing, and they must turn in every tax return and payment on time. EA's are required to do extensive ongoing training every year. Their training usually exceeds the IRS' basic requirements.

EA's are required to abide by the provisions and ethical standards of the Department of the Treasury's Circular 230.

EA's have a limited client confidentiality privilege under the law, usually for audits and collections.

Because of the high requirements, there are fewer than 50,000 IRS Enrolled Agents in the entire county. The American institute of CPAs has nearly 400,000 members.

Therapist, Psychologist, Counselor

Money and therapy can be surprisingly intertwined. You may want to engage a therapist to help you if you have received instant money, if you are going through a divorce, and of course, if you need help to work through any number of modern-day challenges.

This is a safe, confidential place to talk about your life and anything that may be confusing, painful, or uncomfortable. They help you heal and find out how to best handle your life and work through your problems.

There are many different choices and types of therapy, and you need to research based on your particular issue and their expertise.

As you have read, there are many different professionals you might want to consult with to help you make decisions that are necessary in order to move forward and make good decisions.

16.

Conclusion: Start Now

The Seven Steps to Wealthy, Healthy Money and your financial long game:

1. Take inventory of your assets.

2. Check your income, and add it up.

3. Check your expenses from the last 3 or 6 months. Find the money to do what you want and to get what you need.

4. Allocate the income you make each payday to

living expenses and savings. Use a percentage, so that at time of payment you can make the required payments.

5. Invest by paying attention to time horizon (which is a means to measure the time you want, need or have before an event), yield, and risk.

6. Find a Registered Investment Advisor or CFP to help you achieve your goals when you are ready.

7. Have fun!

Don't just try, do. It can be hard, but there are easy ways to get out of your own way. To succeed, there are three words to eliminate from your vocabulary. You will be surprised how changing your vocabulary will change your thinking, which in turn, will change your future.

Words are powerful. What you tell yourself will become what you believe. Our brain only answers the question we pose. If you ask negative based questions, you will get negative answers. Words can empower you.

If your intentions are positive, you will grow automatically. On the other hand, if you come from fear, you will not.

The subconscious mind learns by repetition, so word habits are a powerful way to reprogram it to align with your desires. The subconscious mind has far greater power than the conscious mind, and it is the conscious mind that must initiate change. There are hundreds of books on this subject, but for brevity here are the three-negative word that you can start eliminating from your vocabulary today:

1. Should

Whenever you state, "I should," you speak as though there is external authority acting over you, which ironically creates immediate resistance and denial. This sets you up for an unconscious rebellion.

When you say "I should," or "I have to," stop and take notice. Now ask: "Do I want to do this or not?" If you do, then you can restate "should" as "I want to." If you don't, then you can also state that choice clearly in your mind. Consciously change all *should*s into *want* or *choose*.

2. Can't

Saying "I can't" sends the subconscious mind searching for supporting evidence. The mind then will supply you with all the reasons you can't because the subconscious will never fail you. The more you use "I can't," the more you will perceive and experience limitations.

I remember being told *can't* was not a word, and I was not allowed to use it. Can't will only defeat you.

When you say "I can't," pause and consider why. You

may be afraid or feel unequal to the task. You may remember past unsuccessful attempt or, think of current circumstances that prevent action. After noticing what is going on, turn the "I can't" into the past and say "I couldn't then, but I now can." Now you leave yourself open for new ways to succeed.

3. Try

Saying "I'll try" is weak. "I'll try" implies "I may not succeed." So, when you say you'll try, you are setting yourself up for failure. For example, when you say, "I'll try to lose weight," it really means, "losing weight is very difficult for me and I might not be able to."

Whenever you catch yourself saying, "I'll try," stop and decide what your real intention is. Then either commit one way or another: "I will" or "I won't." Be honest with yourself and you will side-step multiple failures. When you commit to others, either say "no" or "I'll do my best." Mean it.

Investing Glossary

Accrued Interest - Interest accrued on a bond since the last interest payment was made. The buyer of the bond pays the market price plus accrued interest.

Accumulation Plan - A plan for the systematic accumulation of mutual fund shares through periodic investments and reinvestments of income dividends and capital gains distributions.

Active Management - An investment strategy of actively buying and selling investments in an attempt to beat the return of the broad stock market (or another benchmark). Note: academics have reviewed historical fund performance data and found that few active mutual fund managers have been able to consistently achieve better investment returns than the broad stock market.

AMEX - The American Stock Exchange, located in New York City.

Annualized Return - The annualized return (not to be confused with average return) is a geometric average return that takes into account compounding during the year.

Appreciation - The increase in value of an asset.

Arbitrage - Dealing in different markets. Example: Buying on one exchange like the New York Stock

Exchange while simultaneously selling short on another exchange Nasdaq or the American Stock Exchange at a higher price.

Asked Price - The price asked for a security offered for sale. Quoted, bid, and asked prices are wholesale prices for interdealer trading and do not represent prices for the public.

Asset Allocation - The proportions dedicated to asset classes (bonds, domestic stocks, international stocks, etc.) across an investor's portfolio. An asset allocation strategy should be based on an investor's willingness and ability to take risk.

Asset Class - An investment category such as bonds, stocks, real estate, and cash. More specifically, asset classes can identify a specific subset of investments; for example, instead of simply classifying an investment as a bond, the investment can be labeled as a long-term U.S. Government bond.

Auction Mark - Dealings on a securities exchange where a two-way auction is continuously in effect.

Authorized Stock - The total number of shares of stock authorized for issue by a company's shareholders.

Bear - One who believes the stock market will decline. A once popular blood sport, Bull and Bear fighting is thought to give the market trends their names. Bears fight by swiping downward; bulls fight by thrusting up their horns. Neither the bulls nor the bears were consulted before their images were appropriated by Wall Street.

Bear Market - A declining stock market.

Benchmark - An Index for which investment performance can be compared. Investors often compare the performance of their stocks or mutual funds to the Dow Jones Industrial Average to see if they are outperforming or underperforming the market.

Blue Chip - A company known nationally for the quality as well as a wide acceptance of its products or services and for its ability to make money and pay dividends. Examples include Disney, GE, Intel, Visa, and Walmart.

Bond - Basically, an IOU or promissory note of a corporation, usually issued in multiples of $1,000. It is an investment in a company, government, or other entity's debt in which an investor gives the entity money, and in exchange the entity pays the investor interest at fixed time intervals and/or repays the principal at a later date. Investors, may buy a bond from the U.S. Government, U.S. Government Agencies, Corporations, international governments, and as well as several other entities.

Bull - One who believes the stock market will rise. See

"Bear" for a brief history of these terms.

Bull Market - An advancing stock market.

Call - An option to buy a specified number of shares of a certain security at a definite price within a specified period of time.

Callable - A bond issue, all or part of which may be redeemed by the issuing corporation under definite conditions before maturity. The term also applies to preferred shares, which may be redeemed by the issuing corporation.

Capital Gain or Capital Loss - Profit or loss from the sale of a capital asset. A capital gain, under current federal income tax laws, may be either short-term (six months or less) or long-term (more than six months). Capital gains are taxed at the reporting individual's full income tax rate. Since 1987, losses are deductible $3,000 per year.

Capital Market - The market that deals in long-term securities issues of both debt and equity.

Capital Shares - Shares to which all gains or losses accrue and which have no claim on dividends. Refers only to a dual or leveraged-type closed-end investment company.

Capital Stock - All shares representing ownership of a business, including preferred and common.

Capitalization - Total amount of the various securities issued by a corporation. Capitalization may include bonds, debentures, preferred and common stock, and surplus.

Cash flow - Cash distributions from an investment. Negative cash flow occurs when expenses exceed income.

Certified Financial Planner (CFP) - A designation granted by the Certified Financial Board to individuals who complete a six-part curriculum in financial planning (including risk management, investments, tax planning, employee benefits, and estate planning).

Correlation - A statistical measurement showing how a stock or fund performs relative to another. Perfect positive correlation implies that as one stock or fund moves, either up or down, the other will move in the same direction. Alternatively, perfect negative correlation means that if one stock or fund moves up, the other will move down, or vice versa.

Diversification - Investing in a variety of investments with the goal of lowering the portfolio's risk by minimizing its exposure to any one stock, industry, asset class, or country. The intention of diversification is to eliminate company-specific risk (i.e. unsystematic risk).

ERISA - Employee Retirement Income Security Act of

1974. Created to set minimum standards for most voluntarily established pension and health plans in private industry to provide protection for individuals in these plans.

Exchange Traded Funds (ETFs) - Most commonly a fund whose goal is to track the performance of an index such as the Dow Jones Industrial Average. An ETF is similar to a mutual fund in that it typically contains many individual underlying holdings. In some ways, however, it is different than a mutual fund and more like a stock in that it can have options and can be bought and sold short throughout the trading day.

Emerging Markets Stock - Shares in the financial markets of a single, or a group, of developing countries.

Equity - An ownership interest; also, referred to as stock.

Federal Deposit Insurance Corporation (FDIC) - The federal agency that insures deposits of up to $250,000 in member banks. The FDIC was created by the Banking Act of 1933 after the Great Depression to restore trust in the American banking system. The insurance limit was initially $2,500 per ownership category. Since the passage of the Dodd-Frank Act in 2011, the FDIC insures deposits in member banks up to $250,000 per ownership category.

Fiduciary - A person who holds a legal or ethical

relationship of trust with one or more other parties. Typically, a fiduciary prudently takes care of money or other assets for another person. A fiduciary makes all choices best for their clients has a higher standard than suitability.

FINRA - Is dedicated to investor protection and market integrity through effective and efficient regulation of the securities industry. (Financial Industry Regulatory Authority). An organization authorized by congress to protect America's investors by making sure the broker dealer industry operates fairly and honestly. This allows you to check on your broker dealer or representative. Go to www.finra.org.

Index Fund - A type of fund designed to track a market index such as the S&P 500 Index. The purpose of an index is to provide broad market exposure with low operating expenses and low turnover.

Inflation - Rising prices for goods and services. In years of inflation, it costs more to purchase a similar item than it did the year before. The opposite of inflation is deflation, in which it costs fewer dollars to purchase a similar item that it did the year before.

International Stock - Shares in companies located outside the United States.

Large-Cap Stock - A stock with a market capitalization (see definition below) value of typically more than $10 billion. Large cap is a common abbreviation.

Market Capitalization - The market value of a publicly traded company. The market capitalization is a value placed on a company that is based on its total number of shares and market price per share. The investment community uses this figure (as opposed to sales or total asset figures) to determine a company's size. A common abbreviation is "market cap."

Maturity - The time remaining on the life of a financial instrument, commonly a bond or certificate. Maturity often is used in the context of a maturity date, which is the date when a bond's final payment is due.

Mutual Fund - An individual holding where money is pooled together from thousands of investors in order to buy stocks, bonds, or other securities. One of the main advantages of owning mutual funds is that they give small investors access to diversified portfolios which would be difficult to create with a small amount of money. Each shareholder participates proportionally in the gain or loss of the fund.

Passive Management - An investment strategy that minimizes buying and selling investments. Passive strategies often attempt to mimic the performance of an index such as the S&P 500 or Dow Jones Industrial Average. Passive managers seek to minimize costs and avoid unnecessary risk.

Real Estate Investment Trusts (REITs) - An investment (either through properties or mortgages) in one or more forms of real estate such as commercial, industrial, or residential real estate. REITs trade similarly to a stock or Exchange Traded Fund (ETF) and often trade on major exchanges like the New York Stock Exchange.

Recession - A natural part of the economic cycle in which the economy shrinks. Technically, a recession is defined as two or more quarters (6 months) of negative economic growth.

Risk - The chance that an investment's actual return will be different than what is expected. Risk includes the possibility of losing some or all of the original investment. Risk is often measured with standard deviation which quantifies the amount of volatility in investment returns.

Risk Tolerance - The amount of uncertainty (including potential losses) an investor is willing to accept in their investment strategy.

S&P 500 - A stock market index comprised of 500 of some of the largest U.S. companies. It is often used as a gauge of the U.S. stock market.

Share - An ownership in a corporation or financial asset. Being a shareholder entitles the possessor to a proportional distribution in profits, if any are declared, in the form of dividends.

Short term Debt - Any financial obligations that is due within a 12-month period.

Small-Cap Stock - A stock with a market capitalization value of typically between $2 billion and $300 million. Small cap is an abbreviation of "small market capitalization."

Standard Deviation - Standard deviation measures the volatility of an investment's return over time. An investment with returns that vary greatly will exhibit higher standard deviation. Standard deviation is used by investors to gauge the amount of expected risk in an investment.

Stock - An investment that represents ownership in a corporation. Being a stockholder or shareholder entitles the possessor to a proportional distribution in profits, if any are declared, in the form of dividends.

Style - The specific asset class exposure of a stock, bond, or mutual fund. For example, Google's stock style is Large Growth, meaning that it is grouped into the asset class of large companies the experience relatively higher growth.

Systematic Risk - The inherent risk of investing in the stock market. Systematic risk cannot be reduced through diversification.

Turnover - A measure of the amount of change in fund holdings per year. Fund turnover can primarily be attributed to buying and selling holdings. Studies have shown that higher turnover typically reduces mutual fund performance.

Value Stock - A stock that trades at a price that is lower than expected given the performance of the company and key performance indicators of the stock itself.

Volatility - An observation of the movement in the price of an investment. For example, if the price of a stock moves up and down rapidly over short time periods, it has high volatility. If the price almost never changes over the same time period, it has low volatility. Volatility typically is measured in standard deviation or variance.

Unsystematic Risk - Individual stock investments contain business risks such as government regulation, or unforeseen employee or factory risks. An investor can reduce this risk by diversifying. Buying hundreds of different stocks in many different types of companies.

Yield - Also known as return. The dividends or interest paid by a company expressed as a percentage of the current price. A stock with a current market value of $20 a share that has paid $1 in dividends in the preceding twelve months is said to return

5%($1.00/$20.00). The current return on a bond is figured the same way.

Zero Corporates - Same as Zero Treasuries (see below) except the issuer is a corporation.

Zero Municipal Bonds - Same as a Zero Treasuries (see below) except the issuer is a state or local government. As such, the interest imputed is nontaxable. Thus, the bonds can be held by taxable investors.

Zero Treasuries - A U.S. Treasury Bond that has had its interest payments "stripped." The investor receives no interest during the life of the bond, but at maturity, he receives the face amount. Since there are no coupon payments, these bonds sell at large discounts from par. The price reacts violently to relatively small changes in prevailing interest rates. They are suitable only for tax-advantaged investors since the IRS imputes interest annually, and the holder must pay income tax on this imputed interest; they could, however, work well in an IRA.

Citations and Further Reading

http://blog.aaii.com/10-common-mistakes-made-with-beneficiary-designations/

http://www.cnlsecurities.com/core/fileparse.php/196/url t/0016405-BDC-Overview-Questions.pdf

https://www.irs.gov/publications/p527/ch03.html

http://www.investopedia.com/terms/r/reit.asp

https://www.reit.com/investing/reit-basics/guide-private-reits

https://en.wikipedia.org/wiki/Retirement

https://www.irs.gov/taxtopics/tc306.html

http://www.fivestarbkg.com/commercial--business-insurance.html

http://www.rainsure.com/homeowners.html

http://blog.aaii.com/10-common-mistakes-made-with-beneficiary-designations/

http://www.businessinsider.com/saving-at-25-vs-saving-at-35-2014-3

http://www.investopedia.com/contributors/82/

https://www.irs.gov/publications/p527/ch03.html

http://www.cnlsecurities.com/core/fileparse.php/196/url t/0016405-BDC-Overview-Questions.pdf

https://www.irs.gov/individuals/international-taxpayers/foreign-earned-income-exclusion

http://www.sandiegouniontribune.com/sdut-how-the-notion-of-retirement-for-workers-took-root-2013dec28-story.html

http://www.huffingtonpost.com/arianna-huffington/its-time-to-retire-our-definition-of-retirement_b_5774878.html

https://en.wikipedia.org/wiki/Retirement

About The Author

Lillian Meyers is the founder and president of Meyers Financial. She holds a Bachelor's Degree in Finance and has a keen focus in matters of taxation, business taxation, and divorce. Ms. Meyers is a graduate of the College for Financial Planning and has often spoken at many company meetings, student workshops, Women in Business seminars, seniors' organizations, church groups, and more. In addition, she has appeared for interviews with newspapers, radio, and magazines, sharing her insight as a financial planning specialist.

Made in United States
Troutdale, OR
11/03/2026

56844530R00159